CLINICAL DEVIATION

THE DEMISE OF A MODERN CLINICAL LAB

A FICTIONAL CASE STUDY

SHADI ASHRAFI, MD

ACKNOWLEDGEMENTS

I would like to acknowledge and thank the following individuals for their support and input toward the completion of this book:

My editor, *David Pope*, for providing extensive assistance and expertise. His support has been invaluable.

Dr. Raymond Franklin, for accommodating me and my pursuit to learn the business side of clinical pathology.

Cindy Kuehn, for providing me with tremendous knowledge regarding laboratory management and operations.

To my dear parents

TABLE OF CONTENTS

FOREWORD

Picasso once said, "Art is a lie that tells the truth." I invite the reader to briefly approach the business of clinical laboratory medicine through the lens of fiction. Such a vantage point may fortify that which is already known, reveal something new, or even arm the reader with a few new tools. My hope is that, when the lens comes off, the view is clearer than it was before, especially on the topic of deviation.

--Shadi Ashrafi, MD

"An ounce of prevention is worth a pound of cure."

– Benjamin Franklin

INTRODUCTION

We just landed on the metaphorical Galapagos Islands with Charles Darwin. Our exploration's task is to see how well the island's species survive, thrive, or decline into extinction, as the case may be.

Darwin stoops down and cries out in a soft enthusiastic voice, "Look over there. It's a young little clinical laboratory!"

"Fascinating!" one of the team's biologists says, observing with his binoculars. "What's the story of this little fellow?"

Darwin replies, "Well, that's up to you to figure out. Observe him for a few weeks, and write me a report."

As we observe this creature, we need to understand its habitat, its interactions, and its constraints.

We also must determine the species' strengths, weaknesses, opportunities, and threats.

In terms of the success of a species, we know that there are some important attributes to look for:

> *Speed & Maneuverability*
>
> *Intelligence & Innovation*
>
> *Sensory Acuity and Foresight*
>
> *Defensiveness*
>
> *Competitiveness*
>
> *Resourcefulness & Adaptability*
>
> *Attractiveness & Progeny*
>
> *Differentiation & Positioning*
>
> *Energy and Movement Efficiency*
>
> *Cooperation (both inter- and intra-species)*

Nature can seem cruel sometimes, tempting the observer to intervene when the subject of study faces obstacles or suffering. But, the way of Darwin is *objective observation*. Tampering with the eco-system to help out a fuzzy animal in need can undermine the research outcome.

In this eco-system, the creatures must survive against many predators, competitors, and harsh environmental conditions.

When our little lab deviates below its peers, it is at grave risk. This is survival of the fittest.

1

Bellagio Surprise

It was a typical hot summer night in Las Vegas. The notorious Vegas strip was flooded with thousands of Fourth of July vacationers. Just beyond the fanfare rested a quaint Mediterranean restaurant inside the Bellagio Hotel, *Todd English's Olives.* It had a beautiful ambiance, with red, orange, and yellow Tiffany-styled stained-glass decor throughout.

The restaurant's smoky setting was complete with a toupee-wearing piano player with bleached teeth and a glittery jacket. He sang covers of Frank Sinatra until closing. Only in Vegas.

In walked a middle-aged Texan couple, Bill and Barb Dunlap. He was an out-of-shape cowboy, with the customary boots, brown cowboy hat and turquoise bolo tie. She had big blond hair and a sexy red dress, accentuating her plastic surgeon's best artwork.

To Bill's annoyance, beyond the patrons' initial glances of amusement, no one paid the Dunlaps much attention. Attention wasn't what he craved, it was relevance. The couple was just a common relic of what the city represented—a playground for characters from all walks of life, from cowboys to Saudi princes, from bikers to reality TV stars.

The lump inside of Bill's sport coat was a box with a surprise diamond necklace. He had purchased it at 70 percent off earlier that day. The Dunlaps were seated at their reserved candlelit table, with nice red velvet seats and perfectly placed silverware. This was to be an anniversary night to remember.

While indulging on smoked mussels and clam appetizers, Bill ordered a porterhouse steak, medium rare, and Barb ordered the roasted Maine lobster *fra diavolo*. His *Jack Daniel's* whiskey and Barb's bottle of *Pinot Grigio* came just as another set of cowboy boots walked quickly toward their table, catching Bill's eye.

"William Dunlap, Jr.?" the older mustached gentleman asked in a husky cowboy voice. The piano music stopped playing, and the restaurant collectively hushed, people staring at the scene.

"I'm Bill. What the hell is this?" He asked in protest, glancing at Barb to see if she was up to something for the occasion.

The man shoved a set of folded blue court documents on Bill's lap. "You've been served. Good luck!" Briskly, the man walked out of the restaurant.

"He got served, folks!" the piano singer announced over the microphone in one of those annoying, cheesy voices. "It looks like someone's going to be washing dishes in the back tonight!" The whole restaurant roared with laughter. This was certainly not the kind of attention Bill had been seeking.

Barb sank in her chair, her face flushed with embarrassment.

Without inspecting them, he swiftly concealed the papers inside his sport coat. "Don't worry, Barb. I'm sure it's nothing," Bill's unnerved voice pleaded while everyone was looking at their table.

"What's going on, Bill?" she asked with a cocktail of concern and anger. "Are we in some sort of trouble?"

"I told you, it's nothing!" Bill said in a barking yet quiet tone, feeling the stares from the other patrons. "Just eat your clams. I'll be right back." He shot back his whiskey and stormed out.

While making his way to the lobby area, Bill uttered under his breath, "Of all the nights and places...my anniversary?" Unable to find a private area to read, Bill entered a nearby restroom and proceeded into the bathroom stall to look through the court papers.

It turns out that Bill's clinical pathology laboratory in Reno was being sued for $50 million as part of a class action lawsuit. The lab was only insured for $25 million. This was a self-inflicted wound, since he had recently cut the insurance coverage amount in order to save a few thousand bucks a year. The lab had run into some quality issues in the past, but this suit was far more than what Bill had ever expected.

His blood pressure hit an all-time high. Splashing his round, sunburned face with cold water, Bill took a deep breath and looked at himself in the mirror, "Bill, Bill, Bill...Look what you've done now! What are you going to tell Barb?"

Back at the table, Barb was defiantly fixing her makeup, thinking that her stunning beauty was the best way to change her table's attention. Bill's porterhouse steak was getting cold, and there was a half-empty bottle of wine on their table.

With hat in hand, Bill returned to the table. Barb tried to act as if nothing had happened, but her eyes told a much different story.

"Let's eat, shall we?" he uttered with unconvincing optimism. He knew the discounted diamond necklace wasn't going to cut it this time.

Later that night, standing on a balcony overlooking the Bellagio's dancing fountains, Bill texted his long-time attorney, Barry Shapiro:

> *Just got sued again, $50 million this time.*
> *See if UltraLabs still wants to acquire us.*

A call came to his cell immediately thereafter. It was Barry. "What in the world happened? Isn't it your anniversary? It must be Mulliger & Jensen's firm."

"Of course it was Mulliger!" Bill yelled in a scathing rebuke. Bill hated paying Barry to hear the obvious.

"Only they would serve people at special events. It's an intimidation tactic. Bill, these guys are vicious ... This isn't good."

"I know, Barry, I know! Anyway, do you think *UltraLabs* would still buy us out?" Bill asked, pulling back his hostile tone a bit.

"Not sure. They may still be turned off to the idea after you rejected their last offer."

"Well Barry, try for me. And I mean ASAP, Monday morning," Bill stated. "I want this in motion," he commanded.

"What should I tell them is your reason for selling?"

"Other opportunities, I'm sick, I'm retiring. Anything!" Bill said impatiently.

"How low are you willing to go on the price?"

"I'd give this thing away right now!" Bill said, half-joking. "Tell you what, Barry. If a good offer comes in, pull the trigger."

"I'll need a power of attorney for while you're on vacation with Barb."

"Do you think it will sell that fast?" Bill asked with an ounce of hope.

"Just in case, I'll e-mail you the form. You fill in the minimum amount you'll accept."

"Fine, fine! Just make this happen, and don't screw it up. I want this thing to go away."

"You got it, Bill," Shapiro replied. "I'm on it. Don't forget to fax me all the papers."

GOING BIG

Bill's career started after college, wildcatting for oil in the panhandle of Texas and Oklahoma. His years of failed ventures seemed always to happen because the odds were against him. He couldn't help but think that keeping this lab was also a gamble. Suddenly, Vegas and his career seemed to be all too similar.

That night in the hotel's junior suite, Bill again washed his face in the fluorescent-lit bathroom. The cheap, rock-hard soap and array of lotions could not soothe his ailment, nor could all the mini-liquors offered in the suite's mini bar.

With all confidence shattered, fear reduced him into a sort of whimpering adolescent. Looking in the mirror he saw a scared, defeated fraction of himself. Deep down Bill sensed this day had been inevitable all along, but the shock of it all was too much to bear. He knew he should have done more to prevent his lab from running amok. He just assumed his confidence and a second wind of luck would prevail.

Standing in the mirror, staring back was the reflection of his father, Dr. William Dunlap, Sr. It was as if he were saying, *"It took you just a few years to destroy what took me a lifetime to build."*

"No!" he yelled at his father's ghost in the mirror. The sound woke Barb in the other room.

"I'm Bill Dunlap!" he loudly slurred in his drunken and delusional state. "I'm going to fight this coward lawyer or die trying!"

Barb came into the doorway, wearing her normal nightgown with a robe, instead of the special anniversary *Frederick's of Hollywood* lingerie she had set aside for the occasion.

"Come on you old cowboy. You've had enough to drink. Let's get you some shut-eye," she said in a soft, disenchanted Southern belle of a voice.

She brought him over to the couch and took off his boots. In the shadows of the room, she took a seat on the loveseat. With more wine in hand, she lit up a cigarette and coldly watched her husband of eight years mumble incoherently until he passed out.

2

The Hunter

Hundreds of miles away, at a private ranch near Grand Tetons National Park, the landscape was exceptionally serene. The morning dew emitted a sweet scent that was enhanced by the fog drifting over the Snake River. A beaver was taking a small break from working on his newly chopped woodpile, while on the horizon, a massive bull elk was responding to a call from the distance carried by the breeze.

Suddenly, without warning, a loud gunshot echoed through the meadow, taking down the elk and scaring all the birds away.

"Got 'em! Damn it all, I got 'em! Ha-ha!" the tall hunter exclaimed excitedly from his hidden vantage point.

This was no one other than Bruce Mulliger, managing partner of *Mulliger & Jensen, LLP*, dubbed the king of medical malpractice for all of Nevada and much of California.

"Well, let's bag him up and take it home," he barked at his well paid hunting guide. This elk trophy was to sit nicely with the others in his game room.

MIAMI SUNSHINE

Thousands of miles away at a luxury Miami Beach hotel conference room, a top New York lawyer was giving a PowerPoint presentation about the latest malpractice litigation tactics and techniques. The fee for the conference was a measly sum compared to the information inside. The gourmet food, delicious; the view of the beach, flawless; the drinks served to cutthroat lawyers, endless.

To top it off, the senior attendees relished the thought that back at their respective work offices, armies of subordinates were slaving thirteen-hour days on their behalf. These minions are usually dealt with slightly less aggression than a hostile witness on the stand. An especially effective filter, assuring the most motivated and brutal associates rise to the top.

"Jensen, how's it going over there?" Mulliger asked from his cell phone, while overlooking the Grand Teton mountain range from the balcony of the Jenny Lake Lodge.

"It's good, my man," Jensen bragged. "Just learning how to shake down pain clinics without a minute in court." Gazing at the swaying palm trees by the shoreline, he added, "The view here is unbelievable!"

"Well, get back to Reno in one piece. You know I hate having both of us out of the office at the same time."

"Did Bill get served yet?" Jensen inquired, sporting his new sunglasses with a cocktail in hand.

"At the Bellagio dinner table, just as planned," Mulliger confirmed with a big grin. He didn't learn this tactic from some weekend seminar; he invented it.

"Ha! I bet his wife liked that," Jensen blurted out, slightly chocking on his drink. "By the way, don't kill all the elk up there; I'm still planning on making my own hunting trip this September."

Mulliger diverted the conversation by inquiring a bit more on the pain clinics. Ultimately, it brought them back to the topic of Bill's lab.

"If it weren't for the fact that these practices were ran so sloppily, our job would actually be hard," Mulliger told Jensen.

"I totally agree!" Jensen said laughing, now with his feet in the pool.

Mulliger continued, "They are running blind. For every 10 practices we successfully sue, there are hundreds who fail to take notice or install safeguards. Our job is to pick off the easiest and weakest lab with the most meat."

Jensen laughed again. He was amused at the analogy, especially considering the topic of his weekend seminar. Ringing in on the discussion Jensen added, "We find the clinical lab—or other medical practice—with the largest insurance coverage and the lowest quality performance and attack relentlessly. It's as simple as that."

"Jensen, this lab is different. I think we are going to get a big payout here. I'll fill you in when we both get back."

MARKETING

Nearly every Nevada resident knows about Mulliger & Jensen. The firm has spent years perfecting the art of advertising to the masses. It started with ads in phone books, bus stops, radio stations, TV commercials, billboards, and so on. Today, the firm has multiple celebrity endorsements, websites, and even mobile apps.

Patients actually download the firm's mobile app, which helps them collect malpractice evidence while at the hospital. Sheer genius!

The goal is to get every doctor to fear them and every citizen in Nevada to think they will strike gold if they retain them. The net result is far more settlements than trials. Being a target of a ferocious lion like Mulliger is enough to make even the largest hospital fold fast.

Hanging in their office are pictures of the partners with the current and past United States presidents, celebrities, and even Jimmy Buffett himself, perhaps the most important celebrity in Nevada.

"Are you a victim of medical malpractice? Want to become a multimillionaire? Call Mulliger & Jensen!" urges the bombshell model on the mid-afternoon commercial. "Don't forget to download our app on the iTunes Store . . . it will help your case!"

The firm spends over 70 percent of its revenues on advertising, and why not? For every case they take on, they average about $50,000 in hard legal costs. What is the take-home for Mulliger and Jensen? Well, they declined to answer on a local news interview, but it's probably in a trust in the Caymans anyway, which they frequent in one of their corporate jets.

Needless to say, Mulliger had immense influence and resources. The odds always seemed to be in his favor.

MULLIGER & JENSEN, LLP

Back at the Jenny Lake Lodge, Bruce Mulliger enjoyed his view of the Grand Teton mountain range while smoking a hand-rolled Cuban and sipping a glass of brandy. The curious thing about Mulliger was that he graduated from UNLV, a second-tier school, at the middle of his class. He never really cared about anything other than making big malpractice wins.

While in law school, he worked for a private investigator that taught young Mulliger how to hunt, both literally and figuratively. Mulliger's firm ran just like a CIA outpost, with intel, deception and skill.

Michael Jensen, his partner, was a top graduate from Stanford. Mulliger took him under his wing because of his brains and connections, but mostly because of his access to Silicon Valley money. Together, they approached investors to fund big, juicy lawsuits. Combined with Mulliger's cunning tactics, the firm became a towering regional powerhouse.

BARRY SHAPIRO, ESQ.

When the lab gets sued for malpractice, it must hire a defense attorney. If you follow the money, it's obvious that there is more in the business of suing than in defending the sued.

If Mulliger & Jensen wins the $50 million malpractice suit against Bill's lab, the firm walks away with half of the award. Yet, Bill's defense attorney, Shapiro, gets a mere $200 an hour for defending the case. Which side has more financial incentive to be as ruthless and cunning as possible? Who most likely has the better arsenal of resources?

Mulliger is prepared to call the world's top clinical pathologists, psychiatrists, and even celebrities to testify. All witnesses get personal acting coaches to amplify the influence over the jury. Barry Shapiro has nothing close up his sleeve.

In comparison to Bruce Mulliger, Barry Shapiro paled. His face turned red during emotional confrontations, while Mulliger was actually the most relaxed in such moments. Mulliger hated amicable cases and despised the uneventful; so much so, that in such cases, he heightened the drama by rattling his opponent. His first question in every meeting usually goes something like...

"My only question for you today is, would you like to make the settlement in one lump sum, or in payments?"

Who knows why Bill would ever let down his guard to such a predator.

3

Paper Trail of a Mega-Lab

New York City in June 2004 was a goldmine for *UltraLabs'* founder and CEO, Raj Pamalu. Nothing could be more exhilarating to a son of poor immigrants than to ring the bell at the New York Stock Exchange (NYSE) for a company that he personally built from the ground up.

The company started out as a small, regional lab in Seattle. Today, it operates in thirteen different countries, employing over 25,000 people and generating hundreds of millions of dollars in profits to its shareholders each quarter. Its balance sheet shows billions in assets, including equipment, patents, lands, and plenty of cash. Every year, the company raises a few billion dollars in debt to fund another buyout of a cluster of labs in select geographic locations.

Raj's paycheck makes Bill's salary look like a restaurant tip. Last year, he cleared $23 million in stock options, on top of his $5 million salary.

At the big event, he told reporters, "*UltraLabs* wasn't always a mega lab. Its ascent came from a growth model that was ever so slightly better than the pack.

"We are only here because each test costs us just a little bit less than our competitors," he bragged to the interested crowd around him.

"Our quality is superior, too. We preach and practice *Lean Sigma* and Total Quality Management (*TQM*) like it was our religion," he said with conviction. "It is embedded in our culture."

"What about all the small- and medium- sized labs you put out of business?" a reporter inquired.

"They spend their profits while we reinvest ours. They are wasteful and we are *Lean*. In this country we get rewarded for raising the bar", Raj said, defending himself.

Raj's beautifully dressed wife and children stood behind him, albeit slightly camera shy.

"What do you think, Mrs. Pamalu?" the reporter asked. Raj clinched his teeth that the reporter was putting his wife on the spot on live television.

"*UltraLabs* employs thousands, and saves countless lives by being the best at what it does. We should make no apology for our success," she said with a smile and jab at the same time.

"Okay, no more questions!" Raj commanded while turning around to celebrate with his entourage of early investors. They had stuck by Raj and invested in his aggressive quality and acquisition strategies.

With many new public investors piling in cash, *UltraLabs*' board was now free to do more than just buy labs. It was able to actually change the frontier of the American clinical lab industry altogether.

In a private memo to his executive team, Raj reiterated his strategy:

ULTRALABS EXECUTIVE MEMORANDUM

HOW WE ARE TO ELIMINATE SMALL COMPETITORS FROM DESIRED MARKETS

A) PRICE WARS: WE ARE THE 'WALMART' OF CLINICAL LABS

If we are not dominant in a particular market, we need to flood it with low-priced test menus, even if at a loss. Once the customers defect to us and we are the market's leader, we can bring the prices back up again.

Our advantages are scalability, automation and capital reserves. We can afford to have a price war; they cannot. With depleted revenues, eventually the small lab will collapse.

B) INNOVATION ARMS RACE

We must buy and create more clinical lab intellectual property that leads the industry in test speed, quality, and clarity. This forces our smaller competitors to adapt at a break-neck speed, which is more costly than they can bear. Their aging capacity, low quality and slow speed all work to deteriorate their customer base further.

C) COURT FRIENDS IN HIGH PLACES

We golf with the industry's regulators and association heads; while all the small labs get is association brochures, membership dues, audits and an occasional seminar. We receive preferential treatment and protections; while they get endless red tape. In the name of patient care, we lobby for higher quality standards, more mandatory audits, employee certifications, and required quality systems. Basically, we push for anything that favors big labs over the small ones.

D) LEAVE THEM THE LEFTOVERS

The only defense for small labs is to take on risky test menus, outdated analyzer equipment, and less-trained employees. Further, we forgo undesired demographics and regions. This will lead them in a dangerous trajectory. When they are reduced to a boutique lab, their collective threat to us becomes neutralized.

E) BRAIN DRAIN POACHING

We can induce an engineered *brain drain* by poaching their key certified staff, even if at an initial loss. We know these employees are unhappy, underpaid, and have inferior benefits and training compared to ours. The small lab can hardly afford to provide comparable working conditions, and we must lure the best to our side. The lab, without top skilled talent, is thereby neutralized.

F) ACQUISITION

From time to time, we may find a smaller lab with long-term contracts that we can buy out at a bargain. Usually these deals are a hassle, but often this is the easiest way to secure new market share.

G) THANKS FOR ALL THE REFERENCE VOLUME!

Our wholesale test prices must be equal to or lower than the small lab's internal cost. With superior quality and consistency, we economically pressure them to send their test volume to our central processing labs. It can be considered a victory when we have dominated a market this way.

H) SALVAGING THE FALLOUT

If possible, the discounted assets of failed small labs should be salvaged. Valuable analyzers sold at a bankruptcy court's auction block can be picked up for a fraction of the cost; and laid-off employees, whose résumés show up on our fax machines, can be hired at a discount as well.

When this memo was leaked to a prominent anti-corporate reporter, she wrote about how *UltraLabs* and other mega-labs were dangerous for small- and medium-sized labs that couldn't keep up with the rapid industry-wide changes. However, she did acquiesce that the resulting quality improvements and price decreases were great for the patients and overall industry standards. She wrote:

> ...All three measures of quality have been improved: Faster turnaround times, Accurate test results, and Clearer communication to ordering physicians; all at a lower cost. Perhaps we really do need more 'Walmarts of medicine'....

At the *UltraLabs* party, standing with Raj was Carlos DePaul, the top acquisitions manager that had carried out Raj's full frontal strategy leading up to the IPO.

Reno, Nevada was one place *UltraLabs* had not yet penetrated. Bill's lab was a prime target, so Carlos offered a bid. Bill countered with a price much higher, but Carlos didn't take the bait. When Raj learned of the failed acquisition, he personally emailed Bill:

Dear Bill,

I regret that we couldn't agree on the price. Should you change your mind, you know our number. Nonetheless, we are excited to compete with your little lab in full force later this year.

-Raj Pamalu, Chairman and CEO

UltraLabs

4

Yosemite Descent

A distinctive purple glow illuminated the cliff wall of Yosemite Valley. It was sunset, and a waterfall sparkled in the panorama. This was heaven itself.

Perched up on the cliff, Peter McGuire set up a vertical camp with a few of his mountain-climbing friends. The hanging tent was supported by expensive *REI* gear wedged into the cliff rock. With the slightest mistake, the tent would fall, over 1,500 feet to be exact.

Peter was built for this; eating freeze-dried food while swinging like a bat with his friends in paradise. He took it all in like a kid at *Disneyland*.

Peter's climbing friends spent their lives hitchhiking in different countries and living in hostels. Peter had a good job and slept on a suburban bed every night, except for this weekend, of course. He was the only one among his climbing buddies without a beard, but he was no less manly. They liked to call him "pretty boy" to rub in the perceived noose on his life relative to theirs.

Although he was in his element, Peter seemed a bit aloof and heavy. His hanging bunkmate and best friend, Jesse, asked what was wrong.

"Everything and nothing," Peter answered with a sigh. "I spend my life in the lab. Since my job pays well and I can support my family, you may think I'd be happy."

"So, what's the matter? The corporate world not treating you well?" Jesse asked with his hands locked together behind his head.

"Something like that Jess. Tomorrow, I will descend from Yosemite Valley into hell—the city of Reno," Peter complained. "I will run tests all day, over and over, while staring at the clock . . . *pipette out of the patient sample tube, pipette into the reagent cartridge, insert into the analyzer, and repeat* . . . three billion times a day. And then, Jesse, I will die—die miserable.

"I have only so many more tests left in me," Peter continued. "Then, I will be disposed of, just like the used cartridges I throw out. I am a cog in the wheel, or maybe more like a mouse on the wheel. My only contribution in this world is measured by my boss, who can't even remember my name, and who is constantly trying to replace me with an automation machine."

"Why don't you find something else to do for a living?" Jesse asked, searching for a quick solution.

"What? Go back to school for a job that makes a fraction of my current income? How will I afford weekends like this?"

"Well, you could always change your name and run away with us," Jesse said, rolling toward his friend.

"I think I may have no choice."

"What are you talking about, you drama queen?" Jesse laughed back.

"I messed up at work a few months back."

"Really? So what happened?"

"I've just been so distracted lately," Peter confided. "I haven't told anybody about this yet, but this guy from a big law firm told me to get ready for a deposition. You know, where they grill you in some conference room while your being videotaped. I think I'm screwed."

"Was it that *Mulliger & Jensen* firm that advertises everywhere?" Jesse asked.

Surprised, Peter answered back, "Yes, as a mater of fact it was. How did you know?"

"You're screwed!" he answered back with cynical conviction.

Last fall, while working up cardiac enzymes, Peter neglected to call the clinician to report critical elevations of troponins. The analyzer had flagged multiple results, but since no call was made, the ordering physician assumed the results were normal. A big mistake!

"So did anyone actually get hurt?" Jesse asked with concern.

"Put it this way: I think twenty-two people may be suing the lab because of me, Jesse. But even worse, this was the second time this very mistake has happened. We were nearly shut down by our regulator, *CLIA!*"

"Why were you so distracted?" Jesse inquired.

"I was distracted, bored, unmotivated, all of the above. Working at the lab is worse than a post office, and employees are getting short-changed all the time. I mean, they've even cancelled our Christmas party this year."

"So, is this some cost-cutting nonsense or what?"

"Kind of, yes," Peter responded. "But it's more about the complete chaos, combined with the monotony we go through. Nobody wants to be there, nobody is loyal, and it's turning out to be a cesspool of screw ups."

Jesse chimed in, "The rich get richer, and the poor get poorer, right?" Jesse was part of a movement of global travelers getting off the grid as a sort of protest to corporate America, or escapism, depending on one's point of view.

"Exactly," Peter agreed. "This Bill guy that owns the place bought a brand new Escalade the day he laid off a few of my co-workers. I guess he needed the extra space for his fat ass." They both started laughing.

"Quiet down over there girls!" someone in the tent next to them yelled out.

"I'm just saying," Peter continued in a forced whisper, "if they gave us a bone here and there, we would be so much more loyal. Our equipment is aging, our pay is shrinking, and we are all on the edge.

"What If I told you I didn't pack any food for you for this trip? Or what if I said that I got you cheap climbing equipment so I could go out and buy a new Cadillac?"

"I'd kill you!" Jesse retorted.

"I don't think the error was my fault," Peter said quietly. "When those jerk lawyers ask me, I will tell them it was the greedy management's fault!" Peter exclaimed with deep emotion.

Leaving the conversation there, they both stared at the stars through the tent screen in silence. An owl sang the climbers to sleep under the Milky Way, and Peter finally succumbed to its magical trance.

The next morning, he began his descent down the cliff to return back to Reno, leaving his mates behind. "Have fun hiking Kauai, guys!" he yelled.

"Drive home safe, pretty boy!" Jesse shouted back.

After a few days of pipette shuffling, Peter knew he would get over it; he always did. But he had a picture of Yosemite on his personal wall at work to inspire daydreams.

5

Welcome to Reno

There probably isn't a worse way to awaken from a Sunday afternoon nap than to hear a pilot utter the following words over the intercom, "Hello, folks! On behalf of everyone here at the airline, I'd like to welcome you to the great city of Reno, Nevada."

Jacob Simmons was descending on Reno to see if Bill Dunlap's lab was worth acquiring. He was a mergers and acquisitions (M&A) consultant for a big-four accounting firm.

M&A is a "big fish eat little fish" game, and Jacob was simply an agent to the shark—*UltraLabs*. His accounting firm was eying a long-term contract with *UltraLabs*, and it naturally sent the best available M&A star for the job, Jacob Simmons.

Perfectly accustomed to last-minute engagements, Jacob already had his aluminum–plated travel suitcase packed and ready for the occasion. His firm just sent his *Blackberry* an itinerary, and he was soon waiting in the airport sky lounge, reading the *Wall Street Journal.*

This was his first clinical laboratory. Jacob usually audited biotech start-ups or regional hospitals for *Kaiser Permanente* in California. It didn't really matter to him what the business was, he was so good at auditing and valuating businesses that it became routine, mundane, and elementary.

He was like a grandmaster chess player, perpetually stuck in a game of checkers. Yet, the pay was a definite means to other ends. Reno was just a short drive from Lake Tahoe, and he had his sights set on a long fishing weekend, where he could afford to spare no expense.

In order to impress *UltraLabs*, Jacob promised to audit Bill Dunlap's lab first thing on Monday morning. The speed of events was partially due to Bill's lawyer, Shapiro, being a fraternity brother of *UltraLabs*' in-house counsel, and partially due to *UltraLabs* wanting to test the accounting firm's hustle.

At first, Jacob's style was slightly insulting to clients. Engagements that usually took weeks for other consultants to complete took Jacob just a few hours. Billing $30,000 for only eight hours of work seemed an incredibly steep fee, but clients paid for the final product, not time invested in the project.

YOUR ROOM KEY

"Sir, here is your room key card and a free $20 slot machine credit," the front desk lady offered in monotone.

"Thanks. I'll let you know if I win," he responded with a smile.

Walking by the endless rows of slot machines, he randomly decided to stop and slide the card in for a game or two. The first few turns ended with nothing. With only $11.50 left on the card, he was about to leave, but the waitress approached and offered him a drink. He ordered a dry martini and consumed the last of the card's value while waiting for his drink, not really looking at the machine, just studying the sea of fellow slot players.

"This is a cash crop," he thought. "For every $1 drink they offer for free, they probably get $45 in revenue." The inner thinking of an accountant is deep and mysterious, or supremely geeky, depending on your point of view.

Walking toward his room, a large floor manager with sideburns and shaded glasses approached and asked why he wasn't staying to gamble more.

"Early morning ahead," he quickly replied without making eye contact.

That night, while dressed in plaid pajamas with a toothbrush in mouth and news anchors yapping in the background, Jacob couldn't help but think about the entire operation of a casino.

A fail-proof business like this was sure to be ridden with shakedowns and power jockeying from commissioners, mobsters, and card counting cheats. What an exciting industry!

Although far from the hospital scene, operating a casino is in many ways less risky than running a small clinical lab, Al Capone guys and all.

6

Parking Lot Appraisal

With a *Starbucks caramel macchiato* in hand, Jacob Simmons slowly pulled into the lab parking lot in his rented *Pontiac Grand Am*, equipped with the expected bare-minimum features and prudently forgettable beige color. To an accountant like Jacob, the only virtue of a car like this was its swift depreciation for tax write-off purposes and low insurance premium because of its low probability of being stolen.

On the first day of an audit, Jacob customarily arrived an hour early to try to get a feel for how the employees arrived to work, in what car and in what order. Jacob profiled employees by their cars as a sort of game. Not everyone likes his method; occasionally security guards knock on his rental car window.

Back when Jacob worked as a fraud auditor, he especially liked to see who drove the *Ferrari* in the parking lot. *'Pride comes before the fall'* was his mantra. And fall they did. Nothing passed him unnoticed, especially a dim-witted, greedy executive, audaciously embezzling company dollars into a parking lot showcase.

While listening to the local morning-talk radio program, he noticed a *Toyota Yaris*, painted with the clinical lab's logo on the side. This was the lab's sole courier car. In a sense, the priority of a company's management is more evident by the prudence of its fleet than the logo or website.

The Y*aris* was built to last, fuel efficient, reliable, and somewhat aesthetically pleasing. It also happened to be the cheapest reliable car money could buy—a good first impression from a business standpoint. If there were two *H2 Hummers* as the lab's fleet, Jacob could practically conclude his appraisal report right then and there.

First to arrive was a white *Lexus RX* SUV with tinted windows and a 'Soccer Mom' sticker on the back. Jacob could tell right away this must be Maria, the lab manager—early to work, well paid, and responsible. The car had bugs plastered to its nose and windshield. She just got back from the long weekend in Los Angeles, visiting family.

Since *Lexus* was a *Toyota* brand, Jacob speculated she must have had some role in the *Yaris* purchase decision. Given her general appearance and demeanor, he suspected that Maria was a typical overstressed manager.

Next came an older *Nissan Sentra*. This car belonged to Lin Wu, a relatively reclusive fellow who played the viola for the *Reno Chamber Orchestra*. The man and the *Sentra* seemed to fit—a car trying to fit in, the driver, uncomfortable amid too much attention.

Jacob suspected that Lin came in early because he liked working alone. His slouch was a telling sign of attitude. Unmotivated employees are never good for the lab's bottom line.

Much of the examination of a lab is based on making a read on employees. The bland ones go unnoticed to some, but not to Jacob. Some of these bland chameleons can be very profitable, demanding less in wages and benefits, and all the while producing more.

In came a muddy, green *Subaru Outback* with a host of stickers on the back window. "What do we have here?" Jacob said to himself.

The car wasn't so much neglected as it was used to its fullest intended purpose. Out came Peter McGuire with a scruffy face and a confident posture. His weekend in Yosemite Valley emboldened him, but the reunion back to work felt like that of a kid bravely approaching a dentist's office.

One bumper sticker read, '*Got Homebrew?*' Jacob had a respect for Peter. His drive seemed good, but he suspected Peter to be either a rebel or a leader. A few of the obscenities from the car's other stickers indicated the former.

LONELY PARKING SPOT

Many other cars came into the lot. While talking business with his manager on the phone, Jacob pondered the empty parking spot that read '*Reserved for Bill*'. This spot was the most coveted, yet most underutilized of the entire lot. Bill Dunlap was the absentee owner of the lab, milking the business while away on a sort of permanent vacation. "How often does Bill come to this lab?" Jacob asked his manager in San Francisco.

"From what Carlos over at *UltraLabs* says, he is an absentee owner looking to cash out," his manager responded, looking at the notes.

Absentee ownership can be a symptom of a sound business that is well managed and requires no babysitting. It can also mean a neglected business that is milked for revenues with minimal reinvestment.

A *Ford Escape* pulled in to the front entrance, and then quickly left. Unknown to Jacob, this was for a delivery of court documents. The lab had also been served legal papers. If *Mulliger & Jensen* had been able to coordinate the service while Jacob was inside, they certainly would have. Arguably, there are a lot of things they would do, if the law would allow.

THE PRIZE

A mega lab is always open to a bargain. The ideal prize is to find a lab with substantial value that is operating inefficiently because of the lack of a few simple improvements. It's like buying a relatively new yet broken-down *Rolls Royce* at a discount, and finding that it only needs a few new spark plugs.

An audit of the lab was needed to avoid making a corporate blunder and also to check the value of the lab for the shareholders. Jacob's visit to the lab was for the sole purpose of kicking the tires.

With the whole cast of employees in place, Jacob walked inside and introduced himself to the secretaries as a consultant there to see Maria Gonzalez. With this *'consultant'* guise, he was at liberty to turn over every stone in the lab to probe for value, hidden liabilities, risks, and inefficiencies.

This lab staff had no real chance to conceal anything against the great Jacob Simmons. His strategy of shock and surprise, along with an acute investigative ability, meant a three-week audit could be concluded before sunset.

7

Maria, Relax!

Early that morning, Maria Gonzalez was interrupted before work by a text message from Bill:

Call me ASAP! Consultant coming today.

Maria had dealt with many external consultants in her career, *CLIA* inspectors, *IRS* auditors, and the so-called 'consultants' (they were usually just sales people with dazzling cost-saving offers that never seemed to exist in reality). But this text was different; it seemed urgent and suspect. She immediately called Bill.

"What's this about a consultant coming today?" Maria asked abruptly.

"He is going to probe everything in the lab from top to bottom, Maria," Bill replied in a hushed, secretive tone. "Give him access to whatever document he asks for, including the financials. And don't mention the lawsuit, if at all possible."

"Lawsuit! What lawsuit?" Maria asked in earnest. "Are you doing another layoff, Bill? I'm a bit worried here!" she said in one of those yelling-whisper tones.

"No. No trouble, just a consultant there to help the business. Please, just tell everyone he was hired by me, and he's there to help everyone out," Bill disingenuously assured.

In a slight panic, she said, "Okay, but I need time to prepare for him…"

"Maria, relax!" Bill interrupted in a louder, stern voice. "He will only be there for a few days. I've got to go. Barb needs me. Give this consultant what he wants."

That ended the conversation.

A habit Bill picked up by watching too many movies was hanging up on people without saying good-bye. In fact, the only person that Bill doesn't hang up on abruptly is Barb. He only tried it once with her, and the result was a series of angry voicemails, ultimately earning him a night on the couch.

When Maria drove into the office early that morning, the drive seemed like an eternity. "Who is this mystery consultant anyway?" she thought. "A lab compliance inspector? A cost cutter? Who?

"No matter. I'm just going to show him what a good lab I have. I give my everything to this place, and no two-bit consultant is going to undermine or judge me."

As Jacob Simmons walked into the reception area, he made copious mental notes of everything. It was as if he was a walking spreadsheet, and every dimension of the laboratory was a line-item entry.

"Good morning," Jacob said cheerfully. "You must be Melissa."

"Yeah, who are you?" the secretary responded with suspicion.

"My name is Jacob Simmons. Bill hired me as a consultant for a few days. I'm here to see Maria. Can you let her know I'm here?"

In her office, Maria was just looking over the newly served court documents Bill mentioned. "$50 million!" she gasped.

"Maria, there is a Mr. Simmons here to see you," Melissa said over the phone intercom.

"Already?" Maria thought. "It's only 8:00 a.m.!"

"Okay, tell him he is going to have to wait!" she barked back in a resentful tone.

Maria frantically shuffled through her papers and tidied up the office. In addition to this consultant abruptly disrupting her morning, she had multiple other issues to deal with.

"Mr. Simmons, she will be a bit. Can I get you some coffee or water or anything?"

Maria eventually met her visitor in the front area. "Hello," Jacob began, "you must be Maria. I've heard such great things about you."

"Yes, and you are?" Maria asked coldly.

"Jacob Simmons. I'm a consultant Bill has hired. Did he tell you I was coming?"

"Yes, he told me."

"Great. I'd like to chat with you first. Can we meet in your office?"

"Right this way."

Of course, Melissa and Sandy noticed the awkward exchange in the reception area and speculated that Jacob worked for the Department of Health. One by one, each of the technologists wandered by to ask them about "that guy". He seemed hyper-focused on analyzing their work when walking by them.

When asked by other employees about who Jacob was, Sandy answered, "We don't know. He said Bill sent him as a consultant. Maria doesn't even know him."

The lab's secretaries had an impressive skill of using Google to search all sorts of things. Melissa typed in 'Jacob Simmons', which pulled up a long list of LinkedIn and Facebook accounts.

"Hey, look at this one," Melissa said, "twenty-three, single... and in a band . . . cute!"

"Type 'consultant' after it!" Sandy shouted across the room, overriding Melissa's ADHD.

The only information listed by the big-four accounting firms was that Jacob Simmons was an auditor. No help at all.

Jacob knew full well that the first rule of pre-acquisition due diligence assignments is discretion. If word gets out that the company is for sale, workers will focus more on updating their résumés than anything else.

Just seven minutes into Jacob and Maria's meeting, the lab's rumor mill had it that Bill hired a cost accountant to see who should get laid off.

8

Welcome to the Lab

The clinical lab is a mysterious facility that more closely resembles a *NASA* space station than a clinic.

When approaching the work area, there is a small, closet-sized space for putting on personal protective equipment (e.g., gown, gloves, and goggles). Then, one can safely open the door and enter the lab.

First is the specimen receiving/processing area. This is where specimens are dropped off to be analyzed. The technologists spend equivalent amounts of time processing and accessioning the specimens and placing them in one of three bins for workup: chemistry, hematology, and microbiology.

Immediately behind the specimen receiving and processing area is the microbiology department. The techs responsible perform diagnostic workups, including culture and sensitivities. They work one shift, 8:00 a.m. to 4:00 p.m.

Requests to work up mycobacteria and fungal organisms are sent to a reference lab (e.g., *Mayo Clinic*). This essentially means outsourcing, a common practice used when the lab has deficiencies in capacity, cost effectiveness, and, sadly, competency.

Microbiology is separated from chemistry and hematology by a small walkway. The microbiology department reeks strongly of sheep's blood agar. Overall, the space is crowded; the *Bactec* instrument appears to intrude on the plating-area workspace. The virology area, although separated from bacteriology only by a sliding door, is difficult to access quickly.

Next to microbiology is the hematology department. The techs responsible for this area perform routine blood tests, including CBCs and coagulation studies. They also work from 8:00 a.m. to 4:00 p.m., with no after-hours specimen testing.

The department that is farthest away from the specimen receiving/processing area is chemistry. The techs responsible perform routine screens and diagnostic workups on blood and body fluid specimens.

It seemed odd to Jacob that the department handling the highest number of specimens is situated so far from the processing area.

Reference chemistry studies are sent to *Mayo*. The chemistry department seems quite roomy and organized. The standard operating procedures (SOPs) are in binders organized in alphabetical order on a bookshelf.

Needless to say, the whole thing was both foreign and familiar to Jacob. He didn't really worry about understanding the particulars of operations, just about finding where things were below standards and needlessly inefficient.

PLAY NICE

After the typical small talk, niceties and quick tour, Jacob moved in with a serious voice and said, "Maria, I'm here to examine this lab from multiple points of view. I'm simply a consultant hired by Bill, so there's no need to worry. Under Bill's direction, I'm going to need to see everything. I have a checklist here. The sooner I get these items completed, the sooner I will be out of your hair."

Maria was furious. "Why didn't you make an appointment, Mr. . . . ?"

"Simmons," Jacob answered without missing a beat. "I'm not sure why Bill had me come without an appointment, but since he sent me here, he is the boss of us both for the day. I guess we are stuck here and have to do what he says."

"Okay, what do you need first?" Maria said with a sigh of contempt.

Jacob took a sip of his warm beverage and said, "I need to start with the financials, of course."

"What do you mean financials? I have a massive stack of invoices, receipts, spreadsheets . . . What exactly are you looking for?"

"You know, the balance sheet, income statement or profit and loss (P&L)," Jacob said in an intentionally condescending manner.

"Well, um, let me see what I can find and bring to you later."

Obviously, Jacob had hit a nerve with Maria, who thought, "Here he is, showing up unannounced, and now he is asking for sensitive financial documents!"

Maria sent Bill a text from under her desk:

> *He wants all the financials. Tell your accountant to bring them by.*

Maria knew full well she could get the financials faster. She just wanted to make things more difficult.

When she finally told Jacob she didn't have anything, he asked if he could simply aim to reconstruct them manually until they came in.

9

Balancing Act

The atmosphere in Maria's office was intense. This was set to be a long day and, probably, a long week. Not even 8:30 a.m. and Maria had a boss to manage, a lawsuit to grapple with, a consultant pestering her, and she hadn't even checked her e-mail!

"Let's start with the balance sheet, shall we?" Jacob asked in a forced upbeat manner. "What does this company have in the bank?"

"I'm not sure, we will have to wait for our next statement to come in the mail."

One of Maria's greatest skills was *stonewalling*.

He retorted, "How much is the lab currently owed, you know, in accounts receivables? By hospitals, patients, insurance companies, etc.?"

"Of course I know what accounts receivables are!" she snapped back. "We will just have to wait to see what the financials say won't we?" she said with a grin.

"Can you get those financials as soon as possible for me?" Jacob asked in earnest.

"Sure," Maria said with a passive-aggressive, phony flight attendant smile. "I'd be happy to."

"What about prepaid stuff, insurance, taxes, leases, etc.?" Jacob asked.

"Why do you need to know that?"

"Because those are considered prepaid expenses and count as current assets. You know, assets that are short term in nature. Also, what are the inventories and supplies in stock?"

"Well, I'm not sure. We have tons of items in stock. Would you like to count them?" Maria asked sarcastically.

This was far from a pleasant consultation. Maria had been put on the spot in a tremendous way. Realizing that her job may be on the line, she toned down her sass and tried to cooperate as amicably as someone in her shoes could.

"What about equipment? What's leased, and what's owned?"

"We have several instruments here. I know the *Coulter LH 500* and *Access 2* are owned. We lease the rest of them."

"Talk to me about depreciation," Jacob said. "How much have you accumulated on the books?"

Maria gave a blank stare.

"Okay, no problem. This is a good start. How much does the lab have in supplies, in furniture, fixtures, and land?"

Now the stare turned into a snarl.

"What about accounts payable? Who do you owe and how much?"

Glaring at the question, Maria slowly and firmly said, "I don't know off the top of my head."

"Okay, do you have any loans on the books?"

"I'm sure we have plenty of loans sir, but I just couldn't tell you the details, because I just don't know."

Jacob's callous objectivity served to be his greatest strength and weakness. Like a computer, he tends to exhibit no emotional response to any tactics; it's just input and output. Don't like it? Oh well. Afraid you're going to lose your job? Oh well. Not the attitude to get many special favors, yet at the end of the day, he gets all the data he wants. What are the raw facts? Take me to them. Let me calculate, confirm, and move on. They may come by blood, sweat, and/or tears, but they are going to be exposed one way or the other.

A shrewd jerk? Yes. But the best jerk for the job, especially with the Maria's of the world. Playing nice isn't always the best way to get information. Keeping a stoic and mysterious presence of authority yields Jacob far more information than being nice.

Investigators, like Jacob Simmons, hit hard and fast leaving everyone confused about what just happened. It's not until after he's long gone that they realize he was even there. This is the best way to collect information vital to the M&A process.

Once people detect someone like Jacob is watching them, they become scripted and concealing. Nobody walks normally when they know they are being studied. No employee gives the appearance of not being a hardworking soldier when a cost-cutting accountant walks through the workplace asking about job descriptions. Job survival is the employee's instinct.

Jacob was not only an unexpected guest; he was also an unwelcome one. Being caught off-guard, Maria had no choice but to show him an exposed lab in all its inglorious flaws. Jacob's interrogation, combined with the lawsuit, all within minutes, severely undermined her composure. Despite her deterrents, it was Maria who was off-balance, not Jacob.

It was her job to hold down the lab with utmost diligence and skill. Through Bill's absenteeism he placed the mantle of leadership into her hands, a secure and indispensible position. Yet, she soon realized Jacob's presence meant such job security could in fact be at risk.

As Jacob's unflinching expeditions for facts continued, Maria began to quiver with emotion; her answers soon became less defensive and more incoherent. The only one playing nice now was Maria.

Finding it hard to disguise her contempt, fear, and confusion, she found herself revealing more than she would if she had prepared. This was exactly what Jacob hoped for.

THE STORY OF THE BALANCE SHEET

When Bill inherited the lab from his father, what exactly did he get? The lab was structured a bit differently than most of the professional partnerships in the industry. *Dunlap Diagnostic Labs,* an LLC (instead of a partnership), was 100 percent owned by Bill's father, Dr. William Dunlap. Part of his will stated that the company ownership interest would be transferred to Bill, Jr., with all the rights and privileges of an owner. At first glance, it may seem that the lab's property is Bill's property, but in fact, it is the LLC entity's property. Bill only owns the share interest in the lab. This means that if the lab were to take out a loan, Bill couldn't just transfer it into his own account and gamble with it. Bill was entitled to select the executive managers (Maria in this case) and withdraw from net proceeds and owner's equity.

The secret enclaves of the accounting universe are based on a mysterious equation, familiar to only a lucky few:

$$\text{ASSETS} = \text{LIABILITIES} + \text{OWNER'S EQUITY}$$

No matter the transaction, the balance sheet must indeed balance out. A loan on one side balances with cash on the other. Expenditure to procure equipment decreases assets and increases assets by the same amount, balancing the equation. If Bill were to inject capital (unlikely as that may be) the owner's equity and cash assets would increase together the same amount.

The line items on the balance sheet are as follows:

Assets	=	Liabilities + Owner's Equity
Current Assets		**Current Liabilities**
Cash		*Accounts Payable*
Accounts Receivable		*Short Term Notes*
-Doubtful Accounts		*Current Portion of Long Term Notes*
Inventory		*Interest Payable*

Temporary Investments	Taxes Payable
Prepaid Expenses	Accrued Payroll
Other Current Assets	Other Current Liabilities
Total Current Assets	Total Current Liabilities
Fixed Assets	Long Term Liabilities
Long Term Investments	Long Term Debt
Land	Deferred Income Taxes
Goodwill	Other Long Term Liabilities
Buildings	Total Long Term Liabilities
-Accumulated Depreciation	
Property, Plant and Equipment	Shareholders' Equity
-Accumulated Depreciation	Capital Stock
Total Net Fixed Assets	Additional Paid in Capital
	Retained Earnings
	Total Shareholders' Equity
Total Assets	Total Liabilities and Equity

The lab *owner's equity* grows in these three ways:

1. The net income increases from operations (most common);

2. The owner invests more capital (additional paid-in capital); and

3. The shares (or partner interest) bought back appreciate.

Bill held on to the business, not because he liked the idea of owning lab equipment, but because he liked receiving distributions (in large corporations, they are known as dividends).

The lab's balance sheet, as kept by Bill's accountant, was not very impressive. Most of the analyzers were leased, not owned; the land and building were leased; the furniture was dated and, virtually worthless (depreciated); and the cash was basically on standby for immediate expenses or withdrawn steadily by Bill in the form of distributions.

Needless to say, the business was Bill's (or more accurately, Barb's) golden egg-laying goose. It was a nice, yet dwindling, asset that Bill wanted to dispose of ASAP, pre-$50 million lawsuit catastrophe.

One summer, Bill called Maria in the middle of the night to settle an immediate gambling debt. She had to drive down and transfer the funds to him *via Western Union*. She had to draw from the company's credit line (creating a liability) to meet payroll.

EGG HUNT

Jacob Simmons was on the hunt for hidden value. If the equipment is owned and worth more than the stated depreciated value, then there could be an above–owner's equity value to scalp. If there are lucrative long-term contracts, they can be taken into account as off-balance-sheet assets.

Star employees and teams are always great value-adders. Some companies are acquired simply for this purpose (e.g., software engineering firms in Silicon Valley). There is no line item on the balance sheet for employees. They are usually a company's best *'elevator asset'* that goes home each night.

A lab's own customer loyalty is perhaps the most important off-balance-sheet asset. It consists of reputation, brand value, contracts, location, customer loyalty, credit ratings, and the like.

Inversely, there are many off-balance-sheet liabilities too, including bad reputation, poor credit rating, unrealized fines, obsolete equipment (beyond the depreciation schedule), lawsuits (as in this case), and other uncovered risks.

What could *UltraLabs* do with some stodgy furniture, a stack of reagents, and a few million in the bank?

This was a strategy play, and Bill's angle was to sell his lab for the value of one thing alone—to get out of the larger corporation's way. Usually, there is a non-compete clause in the sales contract. Bill wouldn't be able to dabble in the pathology business again for five years, a welcome change for both Bill and his employees, presuming they don't lose their jobs.

THE PLIGHT OF THE WORKER

If acquired, the entire lab could be dismantled and simply service the contracts by sending them all out to a central reference lab in Las Vegas, Denver, Sacramento, or Salt Lake City.

"When a door closes, a window opens," the saying goes. The problem is that the window is much smaller than the door.

In the information age of globalization and outsourcing, American workers are constantly feeling the doors shut on them. If the lab staff members get laid off or downsized, the proverbial window means less pay and benefits, more hours, and lack of seniority. The plight of the laboratory professional is causing real friction and, as in Peter's case, has the ability to trump any liability and evaporate any asset the small lab can accumulate.

AGENT OF CHANGE

Jacob is a *de facto* agent to the new wave of an industry forced into a pattern of constant consolidation. Knowing this firsthand, he avoids making friendships with anyone at his subject engagements. The reason is simple: How can you not tell a friend that the winds of change and potential ruin are upon them?

"This is just business, and it's either me or someone else," he told himself. At least, that's what he used to think, before he stopped rationalizing altogether.

If the balance sheet is a net sum of all the positives and negatives, emotionally and perhaps morally, Jacob was running a negative equity deficit; a deviation below humanity.

A Lake Tahoe vacation was a small comfort where he could forget the gap. Everything served as a means to these little pleasures.

During a break, he texted his manager back at the home office:

> *No balance sheet, no real assets turning up...no surprise.*

10

Getting Paid

Jacob was a bit annoyed at Maria's resistance and her ignorance concerning the balance sheet. Although a red flag, it wasn't really much of a big deal since many owners keep their managers in the dark about the full details of the lab anyway.

But Jacob didn't place much weight on the balance sheet's value in the first place, nor did *UltraLabs*. They were looking for the test volume market share, not the relatively minuscule assets of a small lab. The real target of interest to Jacob was the lab's income statement. When assessing the company, he must ask...

How much in revenue comes in?

How much in expenses goes out (and to who)?

And most importantly, what's left over?

"Okay, now I don't suppose you have a recent income statement?" Jacob asked Maria while adjusting his glasses. The question itself was a bit redundant, because without the balance sheet, the chances of her having the income statement were slim.

Sighing with a newfound impatience, Maria snapped back, "Again, I will have to wait for our accountant to send that over."

"Very well, then. Let's just loosely work up last year's statement. The last quarter's . . ."

"Do we really have to do this now?" Maria interrupted. "I have a lot of catching up to do here," she answered like a child trying to negotiate out of vegetables or homework.

"Maria, I'll be as fast as possible, but I have to do this," he responded firmly. "I'll be happy to come back in an hour."

With only mild sympathy for her stressful situation, he wasn't about to let her delay his work.

"No, no . . . let's knock this out now," Maria said with a half-hearted resolve.

"Okay. So, let's start with who pays the lab."

"*Medicare, Medicaid,* private insurance companies, hospitals, and physicians," Maria fired off swiftly.

"What was your revenue last year?"

"A few million, but I'm not sure exactly," she reluctantly said, as if she had surrendered the location of a hidden treasure.

"Fair enough, what about your cost of service?" Jacob asked. " I mean, how much does it cost to run a test, times the total volume of tests?" he clarified. At this point, he wasn't expecting any real accuracy in her answers.

FROM WATERFALLS TO TRICKLING STREAMS

The clinical lab's income statement is like a waterfall with a hundred little straws siphoning off water. The initial water volume is usually the lab's reimbursements, or rather, revenues (accounts receivables on the balance sheet). Insurers want to decrease the flow of water, and everyone else wants a drink of funds that come in (which includes accounts payable on the balance sheet). The aim is to have something left at the bottom; this is the bottom line, or the net income.

Revenues
Cost of Services (Tests Performed)
Gross Profit
Operating Expenses
Selling, General, and Administrative Expenses
Depreciation and Amortization
Other Expenses
Operating Profit

Interest Expense
Other Revenues or Gains
Other Expenses or Losses
Earnings Before Taxes
Income Taxes
Net Income
Withdrawals to Bill's Bank Account
Whatever he leaves goes to Owner's Equity (a balance sheet line item)

When it comes to the financial threats that labs face, the flow of insurer reimbursements takes priority. When there are *Medicare* cuts and *Obama Care* caps, and private insurers are clamping down on claim payments, the lab has to fight tooth and nail to get paid.

There was a time when the lab would get paid for about 99 percent of the insurance claims. Today, it is far less, and the claims take much longer to process. For everyone in the lab, from the owner to the janitor, *shrinking revenues* is a threat to livelihoods.

COST OF SERVICES / TESTS PERFORMED

The fattest and most predominant straw in the lab's waterfall is the cost required for a lab to run a test. Every year, the direct costs (reagents, labor, supplies, reference lab fees per test, etc.) increase. So do the indirect costs, such as the utilities and required costs imposed by associations and regulators (e.g., dry runs or volume-sensitive inspection fees).

Whenever a lab fires up its analyzers to run a test, everyone lines up with a straw. Subtracting all these values from revenues equals the gross profit margin.

Jacob was keen to see this metric because it showed how well the core operation performed as a whole. If the margin was low compared to competitors, then the lab could ramp up efficiency post-acquisition and get an edge. If the margin was too low, it may be beyond repair. To nobody's surprise, the lab's margins were dangerously low.

Every new regulation requires a new expense in order to become compliant. A lab manager is hard-pressed to get a single phone call that doesn't somehow equate to more expenses.

OPERATING EXPENSES

If, for whatever reason, the lab doesn't run any tests (in-house or referenced out) for a given time, it would still have operating costs, though no cost of services/tests. Rent is still due, so are salaries to administrators, Bill, and pathologists. Absent any tests, the lab's technologists are first to go, then the pathologist contracts become terminated, the administrators' hours are cut severely, and eventually, the owners wind down the business, effectively laying themselves off.

Almost everything else, from association dues to janitorial expenses, falls into the operating expenses category. The idea is to segregate overhead from actual testing operations, so as to see how efficiently the lab is operating according to its core purpose: *running tests.*

OTHER EXPENSES, LOSSES OR GAINS

Whenever the lab buys or sells an asset (e.g., an analyzer), it shows up as a capital expense on the income statement (and an asset on the balance sheet). A gain occurs if there is a sale that yields more than what the balance sheet states. A loss occurs when it sells for less (depreciation).

If the lab is forced to pay a fine to regulators or settle a lawsuit, then it is a loss. If Mulliger has his way, the loss that would show up on the lab's income statement is about $25M, after the insurance pays its part. With no viable way to pay, the lab's assets would then be liquidated and the lab shuttered.

INTEREST

Bill's lab had several loans and lines of credit with *Bank of the West* in Reno. The relationship with the bank started to suffer once a few *accounts payable* payments came past due. The lab's *D&B (Dun and Bradstreet)* credit rating slipped, raising the interest rate on the lines of credit. Just last May, the bank even denied the lab's loan request to acquire new equipment.

Interest expense contributes to the cost of capital. When it is high, it is a straw in the waterfall that will take a profitable lab to ruins in no time. Jacob, Bill, and anyone else with an ounce of wisdom know this one lesson: *Never short-change the bank.*

TAXES

Anyone with any experience knows the even more important lesson: *Never <u>ever</u> short-change the IRS.*

If you don't pay the creditors, you get a letter. If you don't pay your employees, you get sued. If you don't pay the bank, you will pay high interest. If you don't pay the *IRS*, you sit in a jail cell.

The *IRS* is the ultimate collector. It takes its share from everything and everyone that makes anything, sells anything, and virtually, does anything. Whatever is left after interest (gross income), the *IRS* gets a share based on the federal tax rate.

Bill and his accounting firm aim to minimize tax liability at every turn. Every expense, and even depreciation, on the income statement is a potential tax write off. To be expected, *UltraLabs* pays a far lower tax rate than Bill's lab does. It borrows for far less, has exponentially more testing volume, and has immense buying power, so its cost per test is far less.

NET INCOME

The last items for consideration are net income and earnings per member (Bill being the only one).

Bill usually leaves very little to retained earnings on the balance sheet. It's not greed but lifestyle—Barb's lifestyle to be more accurate. Bill's dwindling distributions have placed a strain on his relationship with his wife.

Ten-day Mediterranean cruises turned into three-day Catalina Island trips. Even the Bellagio Italian dinner was a downgrade from last year's anniversary getaway at the *Atlantis Resort, Bahamas.*

In a sense, the lab's net income was the only revenue on Bill's personal income statement, and it was usually applied toward past-due credit card balances. Even the diamond necklace he bought for Barb was put on two different credit cards, half and half. Bill rarely reinvested in the lab, which was obvious on almost every level.

The capacity of a lab requires reinvestment. Past-due payments scare off lenders. So, the waterfall is constrained to the investment (reagents, analyzers, labor force, etc.).

Cash flow management is brutal when insurance companies delay payments and when everything the lab buys gets more expensive.

The siphoning force of the waterfall is one to be reckoned with, and Maria felt nearly helpless against it. She worried about making payroll and vendor payments on time. But perhaps, the greatest cause of resentment she had toward Bill and Jacob was their assumption that she was the cause of the problems, the dwindling profits, and quality issues in the lab.

THE BOTTOM LINE: *CHAOS*

As Jacob asked systematically about how much the lab earned and spent, it became apparent that the lab's operations were one big mess. Its net income had dropped down a slippery slope.

The lab seemed like it was getting punished more than a kid sent to fat camp, resorting to tofu on lettuce. The lack of calories (net income) was coming out of the fat reserves (the lab owner's equity and everything else).

It wasn't a pleasant time for Maria or Bill. All the employees noticed, too. Fewer perks, late paychecks, and major skimping on supplies and quality controls were becoming the *new normal* for the lab.

Needless to say, everyone in the lab knew that its very survival was under siege. What kept the lab afloat was its ability to hang on to a few major contracts. Yet, the hospitals, too, were shopping for alternatives.

Quality issues, delays, communication issues, and high prices were deteriorating their confidence in the lab's ability to perform. As soon as all the hospitals and practices caught wind of the suit, Bill knew they would abandon his lab for good.

What could Maria do? What could Bill do? With little foresight, there was no apparent solution, and the lab existed day to day in a fog of chaos.

Jacob suspected that the lab was a *'no-buy'*. However, he did note that, since the main contracts were vulnerable, it was a leverage point for the potential buyer, *UltraLabs*, to use against Bill.

The main rule that Jacob set for giving a *'buy'* rating for a given business was to simply pretend that he had a choice of buying the subject company versus a competitor, and when possible, a publicly traded competitor.

What's safer? Buying Bill's lab for $3 million, or investing the same amount in a health-care index fund, a *Quest Diagnostics, LabCorp,*

UltraLabs, or the like? Obviously, once you own a lab, you are stuck with it because there is no line outside to buy a private little company. The *NYSE* trading floor, on the other hand, had a very long line of brokers looking to pick up *UltraLabs* shares.

Bill's shifty accountant finally dropped off the lab's financials. It's never a good sign when they are shuffled and thrown in a box, but Jacob had seen far worse.

11

Starbucks Audit

Once the official income statement, balance sheet, and tax returns came back, Jacob looked long and hard at them while sitting in Maria's office. The accounting firm that prepared the reports for Bill was based out of a run-down strip mall, the cheapest Reno accountants that money could buy. It was ill-equipped to hide anything from Jacob.

Seeing some red flags, he stood up, holding the box, and said, "Maria, I hope you don't mind if I take these with me for an hour or two?"

"Not at all, please go," she responded, happy to get rid of the pestering accountant intruding on her week.

Jacob jumped into his rental and drove to a nearby *Starbucks*. Noticing in his rearview mirror a black *Lincoln Navigator* trailing him, he scoffed as it parked near his hideous rental car.

"Oh great!" Jacob said to himself. "What is this? The casino tough guys are after me, too? They can have my Pontiac. Whatever!" He laughed, amused by the whole thing.

Sitting at his table, Jacob picked apart every detail, inferring ratios, and patterns. He noticed that the income statements were either erratic, or a cut-and-paste from years past; nothing in between.

Jacob knew he was being watched. Being hyper-observational, he easily detected the obviously misplaced newspaper fumbler, who ordered only water. It was the driver of the *Navigator* who had followed him from the lab.

Jacob abruptly stood up, gathered all his papers and walked over to the man. He sat down at his table without invitation.

"Can I help you?" Jacob asked with no fear or hesitation. This tactic is most useful in taking the upper hand in such situations.

"Depends. Are you Jacob Simmons?" the driver asked with a witty smirk.

"Why are you following me?" Jacob shot back in a tone of accusation.

"My firm has an offer for you," the driver said. "Shall we sit and discuss?"

"Sure, why not?" Jacob said, rolling his eyes at the drama unfolding around him.

Excitement in finding numbers was usual for Jacob, but highly unusual for most other accountants, who were often destined to the mundane. The most they could hope for was a smile from a cute receptionist.

Everyone seemed to have offers for Jacob. He would get calls from New York, Dubai, and Tokyo. Was he world-renowned? Yes. But being followed? This was a first. Not to mention this was an accountant at a *Starbucks* in Reno, not a government agent lounging in luxury in Geneva, Switzerland.

Standing up after the sales pitch, Jacob said, "I'll consider your offer. Now, if you don't mind, I need to get back to my work."

While studying the details of the balance sheet, Jacob noticed something—an unusual asset in the line item 'goodwill'. The asset value was $50,000, but it had been there for years, without much explanation.

Just before Dr. Dunlap's death, the lab acquired a land and mineral lease holdings company out of Oklahoma. It happened back when Bill was wildcatting for oil. Besides the land and mineral lease, the only other asset the company had was a dusty old post-office box.

Dr. Dunlap and his son had a falling out, and purchasing the land with an oil lease was Bill Senior's way of providing his son with a small amount of moral support.

Bill never inquired further about the land because of the raw emotions surrounding its purchase. Anytime his strip mall accountant brought it up, Bill changed the subject.

"Hmmm," Jacob said out loud. "Why would a clinical laboratory in Reno buy an oil company?" He made a call to his old oiler friend from Houston, asking him to dig up the land records and government reports on the property.

As a matter of principle, Jacob let no stone go unturned. This was his edge against the competition. Financial statements are only ink on paper that correspond to some reality elsewhere; a bank account balance here, a title to equipment there. It's the true auditor who can paint a full picture that turns a financial statement into a 3-D story.

Finishing his latté, Jacob returned to the lab to continue his inquisition. He had some line items to check into. He had to verify every bank account balance, every analyzer, the stockpile of supplies, the debts, and so on. Mundane to a normal human, yes, but never to Jacob Simmons. The closer he was to successfully concluding the audit, the closer he would be to his Lake Tahoe retreat.

12

Night at the Reno Chamber Orchestra

Over the years, the lab's brightest employee, Lin Wu, had become quite the musician. As a child, his mother forced him to learn to play violin, and he practiced for hours each day. *Continuous improvement* was her mantra, and she drilled this into his head. He had to be better than yesterday or suffer the consequence—usually double practice sessions.

He resented her pressure, but he found himself excelling at many things beyond the instrument because of it. This eventually led Lin to admire his mother's focus on making him successful.

When Lin went to college, he decided to rebel against his mother, albeit in a subtle way. He ditched the violin and picked up the viola instead, and he took medical technology courses instead of applying to medical school. Such a path afforded him time to pursue his true passion—playing the viola professionally.

A few months before the big lawsuit, Lin was invited to perform semi-professionally. Playing his major solo and duet parts in Mozart's *Sinfonia Concertante* was nothing short of magnificent for Lin. Work was a place to escape from. He would play full-time if he could, but the low pay and few gigs rendered it to be an unforgivable gamble.

A DOUBLE LIFE

Ever searching for a way out, Lin took on gambling for real. It started with website casinos and moved to full binge weekends at the real casinos of Reno. Undisclosed to his wife, Lin had drained his 401(k) three times over the years, but the last time was the worst of them all. The loan he took out against his family savings vaporized in one unlucky night. While seeking to free himself emotionally and financially, he actually became a slave to his habit.

Desperate for alternatives, Lin caught wind of a Wall Street–inspired federal law. It stated that whistle-blowers earn 10 percent of the fines imposed upon their employers. This included *Medicare* fraud.

After learning of the scheme, Lin *Googled* the keyword 'whistle-blower', which led right to the *Mulliger & Jensen iTunes* app.

While playing his part at the concert, his mind was on the presence of a high-profile patron in the audience, now seeing him for the first time in person. This was no one other than Mr. Mulliger himself, dressed in a tuxedo. He was with an exotic South American companion half his age dressed in a stunning white and gold gown. Lin's heart raced, thinking of the immensity of the lab's revenues billed to Medicare over the years.

In his first attempt to collect evidence, Lin was nervous and awkward. His face was red, his hands shook, and his coworkers knew he was not himself. After a few *Valium* pills to calm his nerves and a weekend of watching undercover cop thrillers, he was finally ready for action.

> *First zoom in, then click Record, and let the cameras roll*

...the application's Help feature instructed.

In just two months, Lin had collected over a hundred photos and 20 videos. Was it enough to get a big payout? Only time would tell.

Mulliger was there that night to collect the evidence from him in person. Those were Lin's terms (an adolescent way to show off his viola skills to Mulliger); not that the lawyer could tell the difference between a viola and a violin, or even an oboe for that matter.

Mulliger represented freedom for Lin; freedom from the monotony of the lab, the chew-outs by pathologists or Maria, the judgment from his peers, the constant griping complaints of Peter and the office politics he never played.

Mulliger was the deliverer of freedom to play viola full-time around the world. All the losses of his retirement would be restored, and so too would his life.

Lin had practiced for this piece intensely, feeding off the adrenalin. The reception hall was a bit dull, certainly nothing like the romantic *007* movies Lin had watched to coach him in the dark arts of corporate espionage.

"What did you think of the performance?" Lin asked, wearing his heart on his sleeve.

"Marvelous!" Mulliger responded immediately with charm. "You belong with the *Boston Pops*! I think we should go somewhere private. Let's meet in my car."

Mulliger hated clients. He preferred to have his associates and paralegals work with them instead. But he made exceptions for *white-whale* cases. The threesome met together in his $450,000 custom *Maybach* limousine.

"I have what I promised," Lin said, referring to the evidence.

"Good. Now, are you really sure you want to go through with this?" Mulliger asked. "You will take down this lab and all of its employees, and you will never get a job in the industry again."

"I'm sure, Mr. Mulliger. I want to do this," Lin said with conviction, overselling his enthusiasm, like a willing apprentice to a prospective master.

"Okay, here's the contract as promised," Mulliger said firmly as he handed over a set of papers. "Sign and my notary public here will formalize everything."

Taking the paperwork, Lin read it over and signed with Mulliger's *Montblanc* pen. Mesmerized by its smooth glide and heaviness, Mulliger snagged it back from him.

"Javinia, can you notarize this?" he asked his stunningly beautiful notary.

And then, it was done. Lin handed Mulliger the *USB* drive with the collected evidence.

"What now?" Lin asked with a genuine lack of direction.

He had never actually considered what would happen after this night. So much effort had gone into this moment. Now that it was completed, he was relieved and nervous at the same time. A void of purpose set in.

"Well, Lin, all I can say is, if your evidence is as good as you claim, I would read this *Robb Report* magazine and shop for a few new toys," Mulliger said with a big grin on his face, handing him that month's issue.

As the door of the half million–dollar luxury car closed, Lin stood and watched Mulliger drive away. Once it was out of his star struck view, he gradually began to feel a large wall of guilt weigh over him. He felt cheapened and duped by a pimp of some sort, like he had sold his soul to the devil himself.

He looked down at his viola case in hand. He began to tear up a bit at the contradiction between the hollow feeling of committing betrayal, and the musical instrument that gave him so much fulfillment.

For a flicker of a moment, Lin realized the ramifications of his betrayal to Maria and his coworkers, to Bill, and the lab's very existence.

Clouding over the glimmer of guilt was a storm of pent up anger. "It serves them right for being so horrible to me!" he rationalized to himself. Then, his thoughts moved to, "I'm sure they'll all find other jobs eventually."

Whatever the justification, Lin was far from being in harmony. He prepared himself for the day he was to face the music with the lab, the media, and eventually himself.

On the other hand, Mulliger was in perfect harmony. Laughing over drinks in the back of his limo, he and Javina made fun of almost everything Lin said and did that night. So much for impressing Mulliger.

SHIPWRECK

Now, Mulliger had two fronts of attack prepared for Bill's lab. The malpractice suit, combined with a major *Medicare* fraud / whistle-blower suit, was a formidable force, especially when the assailants were both employees: Peter, the distracted, and Lin, the disgruntled.

Bill was facing the music himself. Years of mismanagement and neglect caused an environment where this situation was perhaps inevitable.

Without a rudder and sail, a drunken captain is sure to run his ship into the rocks. How much easier it is to cause a shipwreck when the crew scuttles it for you. Jacob was on to something when he noted to watch Lin.

13

The Reckoner

On the drive back to the lab, Jacob couldn't help but ask himself what a top M&A auditor was doing wasting time on such a tiny little failing lab. "There must be more to the story," he said to himself.

After returning from the *Starbucks*, Jacob's whole demeanor had changed. Looking at the dismal financial performance of the last five years, Jacob wanted to change the dialogue with Maria.

"What kind of cost and quality controls do you have installed here?" Jacob asked Maria with a concerned expression on his face.

With Maria giving an offended stare, Jacob followed up, "*Six Sigma*, *Lean*, *TQM* . . . you know," he said while gesturing for her to follow his train of thought.

"None. We have many companies that try to sell us the *Six Sigma* systems, but they are too expensive for it to make any sense," she said while biting her nails.

"What is your defect level per million opportunities, or DPMO?" Jacob asked with an intense tone.

Maria shied away from the question, but admitted that it was at least less than ideal.

Jacob sat back in his chair and covered his eyes with his hand, rubbing his forehead. This was absolutely the worst answer, from his point of view. She could have given him a lab full of losses—nothing in the bank, high turnover, and a wall missing—but to not even know the defect rate was indeed the worst of all liabilities, one no balance sheet could quantify.

An awkward pause ensued in the room. It was painful to Maria, who felt deeply embarrassed, especially considering the lawsuit.

TELEPATHY

Basking in this silence, Jacob thought to himself, "They must be getting sued. Why else the rush to sell? She either doesn't know about it, or is concealing it from me."

Under expressed orders not to divulge the suit, Maria excused herself, detecting that he was onto the issue. Before she left, Jacob asked her, "Maria, there's a lawsuit isn't there?"

"Not that I know of," she said while looking down and away. Her body positioned towards the door, leaving quickly.

While she was gone, Jacob immediately called his firm's retained lawyer in the New York office, hoping they were still open. Fortunately, Valerina answered with her nasally Staten

Island accent, *"McCarry, Waldron, and Feinstein?"*

"Valerina, this is Jacob Simmons out of San Francisco. What's your fee to talk to me today?"

"How about $3,000 for the minute," she wittily answered without delay.

"I need a lawsuit search. Nevada, respondent *Dunlap Diagnostic Labs* or William Dunlap.

"Let me work my magic, Jakey," she replied.

While on hold, the Beethoven music was so opposite to her voice that it made him smile. It was relaxing, giving him a little slice of solace for the week. Before the music's natural resonance, bam! She was back on.

"Got it, you small time accountant. It's a $50 million big one, filed in the local county district court on Friday. Just sent you an email."

"What do I owe your genius skill?"

"What do I owe yours, Simmons?" she asked back.

"Flowers are on their way," Jacob said jokingly.

"Yeah, yeah, that's what they all say . . ." she said, hanging up right after.

This was a pivotal point for Jacob. He could either expose Maria then and there, or stay on for the next day to tour the rest of the lab, as he actually liked to do.

Secretly, Jacob loved the engineering and mechanics of things. Financial reports were just paperwork that never really satisfied his appetite for learning about systems and operations.

Maria came back in with coffee in hand. With Jacob sitting in her office with a smile on his face, she knew that he had some new information.

"Maria, what's really going on here?" he asked with a no-nonsense, don't-lie-to-me kind of tone.

COMPOUNDING STRESS

In her work, Maria sustains tremendous pressure to contain costs without compromising patient care. Every day, she and the clinical team bear the burden of complying with multiple regulators, insurers, and private accreditation bodies. There are major labs with which to compete, multiple risks to mitigate, customers to appease, employees to manage, and sophisticated equipment to maintain.

Maria must figure out how to control these issues in order for the lab to survive. The *Lexus*, the salary, and the job security pale in comparison. Bill's neglect of the lab is so different from his father's careful management style. It is sometimes overwhelming to her.

Exposed by this visitor, Maria's hands started to shake a bit.

Jacob took off his glasses and soberly said, "Maria, your lab is going to collapse, and everyone here, including you, will be without a job if you don't do exactly what I'm about to tell you."

"What should I do?" she softly asked, her lips quivering.

"You need to implement a total overhaul of this lab. This place is nothing short of pure chaos. You're the captain and this place is a sinking ship."

Maria's shaking turned into tears; she broke down. After all, it was she who did everything in her power to keep the lab going every day for the last decade. Nobody committed more to the lab than she did.

Jacob stood up and gave her a gentle side hug. He consoled her as he handed her his suit's handkerchief.

Jacob had a rule, he was never to intervene in failing businesses, only to appraise them. But her tears rattled him a bit, tapping a well of compassion he hadn't expressed for years.

"Honestly, it may be too late, Maria, but I'm going to coach you for a few hours on how to save this lab. Everyone out there is depending on you."

He knew it was a long shot, but he felt compelled to help. It was all he could do for a dying cause. Perhaps it was also his form of redemption for a cold and stoic life as an accountant. Added to his personal balance sheet was an entry of a little humanity.

14

Maria

On Memorial Day weekend in 1999, the country club threw its annual catered party for all the members. Maria's catering company worked very hard to land the $144,000 contract. With fresh salmon ordered from Alaska, fresh lobster from Maine, champagne imported from France, Maria had her staff rehearse and her chefs prepare.

Everyone visited the salon just before the event. *Excellence in all things* was Maria's core driver. In the business of catering to high net worth clients, reputation supersedes margins. She only walked away with $4,500 after it was all said and done.

Dr. William Dunlap watched the catering company with awe. He pondered on the implications of such excellence applied to his lab. Observing Maria's cool and calm managerial style, he approached her to inquire further.

"How do you get them to work so well together?" Bill Senior asked with a big smile and genuine expression of interest.

"Carrots and sticks, sir," Maria responded. "Can I get you some more champagne?"

"Of course! The name is Bill Dunlap, and you are?"

"Maria Gonzalez. Here's my business card. We can cater for any event," she said, reverting to her other duty of salesmanship.

Marveling at the professionalism and quality of the food, Bill took interest. He knew the cost of the party, and was astonished that she was able to pull it off so well. Other catering companies were charging double, and with half the quality. His lab was in need of managerial leadership, and he wanted someone like her.

After Dr. Dunlap had her cater for his son's first wedding, the two became good friends. One day, Senior asked her to come by his lab to see what he did. When she walked through to inspect, she was blown away by the sophistication of everything.

"What do you think about running a place like this?"

"Dr. Dunlap, I'm a community college dropout. I wouldn't be qualified."

"I'll personally sponsor your education and teach you exactly how to do it."

The rest was history. Bill Senior put her through school, invited her to intern at the lab by his side, and even invited her to family events, not as the caterer, but as a guest.

On her graduation day, she earned a BS in health-care management and a new career. Bill was there in the audience, sitting next to Maria's family, with an employment contract in hand.

He gave her his office and the keys to the lab. But more importantly, he gave her a new lease on life. She appreciated the feeling of having someone believe in her enough to invest in her career. It reignited something in her that day. She would never let him down, never miss a day of work, and never let a single oversight go to waste. Bill Senior needed someone he could place his utmost trust in, and Maria was his girl.

Several years later, Dr. Dunlap was killed in a tragic auto accident on a trip to Santa Barbara. Maria mourned for months. She had lost a second father. The only one who had really believed in her was now gone.

When Bill Junior discovered he had inherited the lab, he flew into Reno to assess the situation. The first thing he asked was, "How much do I get a month?" This was followed by, "Do I have to do anything?" Basically, that was Bill's style for the years leading up to Jacob's audit.

Maria was still committed to the lab, more than anyone ever was or could be, but Bill Junior was no inspirational figure, no support, and nowhere to be seen.

Once, when he had a big gambling debt to pay, he threatened to fire her if she didn't get him enough to pay it. Maria's response was, "If you fire me, what will Barb do when you foreclose on your mansion?" He hung up on her.

Maria did everything in her power to hold the lab down, but the compounding issues had brought her to a breaking point. Now that Jacob had both exposed the lab's flaws and offered to help, she was extremely motivated to turn the lab around. Failure of this lab would be failure to her deceased father figure, Dr. Dunlap.

15

Crash Course

Despite the lawsuit, Jacob couldn't stand to see Maria and the lab fail without doing something to help. He didn't want to waste his valuable time either, so he asked if she was really committed. Maria was all game. Her tears turned into a sort of burning desire to salvage the lab at any cost. If there was one thing Maria was not, it was a quitter.

LAY IT ON ME

"Okay, Jacob. Lay it on me," she said with a bit of motivated fury in her eyes.

"First, I want you to read this article heading," he said, handing her a printout that read:

It's every laboratory director's nightmare: not enough staff, vendors owed money, and errors

CEO SUMMARY: Lab executives and pathologists have long read about the deteriorating finances at many rural hospitals, along with their struggles to recruit and retain enough skilled laboratory staff.

Now the closure of the laboratory at the 37-bed E.J. Noble Hospital in Gouverneur, New York, can be considered a sign that these long-discussed trends are becoming a reality. In response to the lab's problems, the laboratory director resigned and notified state officials, who closed the lab after an inspection.

—The *Dark Report* Headline, October 2012

Maria sat back in her high-end black leather chair.

"Do you feel any similarities?" Jacob asked rhetorically.

"God, yes. This is exactly what our lab feels like," Maria said, half joking, half serious.

"Why do you think that is, Maria?" Jacob asked, while wiping off the white board, ready to write

128

out her answers. She didn't say anything, so Jacob took the opportunity to assess for her.

MANAGER OF DEVIATION

"Your job is to control deviation and minimize volatility wherever it exists," Jacob stated with lecturing authority. Still emotional, Maria sighed from his tone. Recognizing this, Jacob backed off from his assertiveness.

BUDGET

"Okay, okay. Let's start from the beginning. We have your annual budget and your income statement. What is the deviation between the two?"

"I'm honestly not sure," Maria said in a defeated voice. "I stopped looking once the difference got too big."

"Fair enough. We need to implement a budget strategy. You need to reconcile the two at least once every month. No matter how painful it is to see, you need to address it head-on, or it will get worse."

"Okay," Maria said, writing down on her paper, 'Budget reconciliation monthly.'

Jacob continued, "The most certain way to bankrupt your lab is to go over-budget, year after year," he said while writing 'budget' on the whiteboard.

"The net income converts into a net loss, which shrinks the owner's equity on the balance sheet, which then changes into owner's deficit. Vendors get paid late, if at all, and they stop sending reagents. The slippery slope leads to a *Dark Report* article, citing your lab as a case study.

"The budget is nothing more than a forward-looking income statement, except that it is more detailed, taking into account the divisions of labs, departments, all the way down to a budget for each employee or test menu item.

"When such detail is contemplated, a clearer plan emerges on how to execute. Assumptions

130

are made with a standard allowance for error. In a way, the budget is a lab's way of saying, 'We expect the waterfall to look like this.'"

Maria was ferociously writing notes in her notebook.

"When the budget is off, it is due either to poor planning or poor execution, but it is always a symptom of waste. Most importantly, such an environment becomes a cesspool for errors."

In fact, the correlation between poor financial controls and poor quality are striking. Jacob, alluding to the lawsuit, asked a question that riveted Maria to the core, "How much do errors cost this lab each year?"

Maria looked up. This was the first time she had ever considered herself, rather than Peter, to be part of the cause for the lawsuit.

Jacob continued, "If we were to cost in the error rate and the average annual cost per test, I bet it would be more than the reagent costs or any other component," he said with certainty.

"The goal is to be as lean as possible without jeopardizing patient care. This is a delicate balance, and we are not about to tilt it away from the patient."

"Then, should we invest in a *Six Sigma* program?" she asked, "Because we don't have the money..."

"That depends on Bill, but a lab your size should consider a hybrid."

"What do you mean?" Maria asked, a bit puzzled. For years, the punch lines and cliché of all the *TQM* systems, with their Japanese names, karate belts, and Greek symbols, were a turn off for Maria, but more for the price than the cheesiness. They always seemed too expensive compared to what they saved, and took far too long to roll out.

The cost-benefit analysis she conducted never netted in favor of investment, but this was more attributable to the underinvestment of Bill. He truly would only invest in things if they put out an immediate fire, never thinking about the value of installing a sprinkler system, so to speak.

LEAN/SIGMA

"Sigma is about quality deviation management. *Lean* is about efficient use of resources. I think the two are inseparable," Jacob explained. "I recommend you do both by taking what is important and leaving the rest."

"How exactly do we do that?" Maria asked with genuine curiosity.

"Start with your weakest link," he said intensely. "What is worse here, quality or efficiency?"

"Quality," she immediately replied, with the lawsuit in mind.

"Well, then, let us start with Sigma. It is a system more focused on reducing defect per million than reducing waste, but waste reduction is part of the means. Again, how many errors per million do you have in this lab each year?"

"I have no idea."

"That's the weakness and the root cause of your quality problems. Just like the budget, ignorance is no excuse, Maria. You must know the metrics you are responsible for before you can ever begin improving upon them."

A defect is not just a random anomaly. It is a system failure, which usually can be isolated and identified by a root cause analysis. Most importantly, defects can be systematically quantified and analyzed; they are functions of probability that most managers are ignorant of because either they don't know how to collect error data and aggressively track down root causes, or they don't want to take the time to assess.

The areas in which Sigma digs to find root causes are as follows:

> *Management (Maria)*
>
> *Man (employees)*
>
> *Method (operation manual)*
>
> *Measurement (financial statements, quality reports, etc.)*

Machine (analyzers, IT, etc.)

Material (supplies, reagents, etc.)

Sigma tries to identify what caused a problem. Was it an overstressed manager? A malfunctioning analyzer? Poor training methods? An expired reagent? Or an inaccuracy in the data, so no one could detect the problem? Most notably in the lab, there are three areas of defect: pre-analytic, analytic, and post-analytic. That is, errors before the specimen arrives in the lab, errors that occur at the laboratory during the testing process, and lastly, errors in communicating the results. All of which are counted as defects the lab takes quality responsibility for.

The system is broken down into two categories: process characterization and optimization. The first stages are to define, measure, and analyze process characterization, then to optimize by improving and controlling.

UltraLabs was fanatical about *Six Sigma*, mentioning it a dozen times in its 10-K annual report. A lab of its size is so well stocked with human resources that they can afford to divert people off the lab floor into intensive Sigma training for a month. Bill's small, understaffed lab couldn't dream of such a luxury.

Decreasing the negative variances and deviations between actual and standard defects (any lacking of the three services, test accuracy, clarity, and speed) should be the main goal for every lab—a goal that *Six Sigma* can seriously help.

Above-standard level defects are a symptom of poor controls. For example, Maria hadn't even known about the cause of the twenty-two defective test runs until months after the occurrence, when Mulliger waged a lawsuit. Having no time to run a root cause analysis of her own, it almost seemed like the lab was miles from being controlled, let alone substantially improved.

"Okay, so we need to move on to your second issue: efficiency," Jacob said, writing it out on the white board. "Aside from test results, *waste* is your lab's number one byproduct."

Lean is the activity that aims to eliminate economic waste, or rather, optimize any asset, expense, or opportunity that is underutilized, doing more with less, faster and simpler. Waste areas include expired reagents, idle employees, empty rented square footage, and underutilized equipment (analyzers).

The opportunity cost is the difference between what optimally could be and what sub-optimally is. The idea of continuous improvement is to bridge the gap and, most importantly, start with the largest gap first.

COSTING: ISOLATING WASTE

The income statement is the first place to check for traces of financial waste. To find waste, compare the lab's costs to past statements (if higher or volatile, there is waste) and then compare to industry standards. To stay ahead of the pack, the cost per test must be average or lower.

"You don't know your cost per test, do you?" Jacob asked rhetorically.

Investigating the exact cost per test is the best way to measure the lab's operational efficiency. Management takes the volume of tests run and breaks down the total cost of services/tests to show how each are absorbed and allocated, respectively. When costs deviate above industry standards, or are volatile, the lab needs to implement cost controls to mitigate.

"For example, if your labor costs $1.10 for a particular test instead of $0.82 per test, then you're going to lag behind your competitors. Do you see what I mean?" Jacob said, not waiting for a response. "But if you can get it down to $0.80 by being more efficient, then you can price it below your competitors, or use the savings to invest in more capacity, and so on."

YOU NEED TO TALK TO A PROFESSIONAL

With income statement in hand, Jacob asked Maria, "What is your cost of reagents per test?"

Maria bit her lip with embarrassment. She was the only one in the lab who was supposed to know this metric, and she didn't.

Jacob had finished talking about all this with Maria. He was an accountant who was strangely excited about the whole thing, talking to someone who was emotional and afraid of losing her job.

"You really need to hire a lab quality consultant, Maria. He or she will show you how to implement a culture of quality and efficiency."

"But, Bill said you were a consultant. Aren't you?" she asked with confusion.

"Yes, but not that kind. I wish I could help more, but it's not my specialty. My firm can help, but you have to understand that we are expensive and usually consult with major companies, not smaller labs like yours."

"Then, why on earth are you even here?!" Maria yelled, furious that he was wasting her time.

"Maria, I am here to see if this place is worth acquiring," Jacob said firmly. "I'm only telling you all this because I want to help your odds."

"So, you really think that we are a lost cause, don't you?" she retorted cynically, fuming with hostility.

"Yes, as a matter of fact, I do. I didn't have to stay here to tell you this. If you want, I can leave right now."

"No, no. This is interesting. You come in here, rile everyone up, give me some tokens of wisdom, and leave just like that! How dare you!" she said, upset by his tactics.

"Maria, you're right. I'm sorry to have offended you. You can hate me, but don't hate this information. It's your lab's only lifeline."

Sensing that any more talk about improving the lab would be pointless, Jacob stopped the meeting short. Gathering his things, he said, "Here is a print out of articles I pulled from my firm's database. Study and apply them, and I think you may have a chance. But you should really try to get Bill to invest in a consultant."

Jacob then walked out of the room without making a scene.

After he left, Maria let down her guard and sat quietly in her office for a while to think. Flipping through the pages of articles and book titles, she found a sticky note that read: "Maria, I know you can do this! —Jacob".

Later on that night, she decided to fully indoctrinate herself with the materials so she could save the lab. Feeling inspired, and with a newfound sense of urgency, she called Bill's phone. As usual, it went to voice-mail.

Jacob spent the rest of the day writing up his M&A appraisal report. Tahoe was coming sooner than he thought!

16

It's No Big Deal

Lin and Peter were eating lunch at *Subway* that day. Their usual routine of complaining about work was different recently. No matter how much Peter complained, Lin just deflected everything negative away. He had bigger fish to fry.

"Doesn't this stuff worry you?" Peter asked impatiently.

"The lab is going to do what it is going to do. You just need to have a good plan B," Lin said with a nonchalant air of superiority.

"Did you see that consultant here today?" Peter asked with a bit of worry in his voice.

"Yeah, I did. Probably just another lab inspector. They come all the time."

"Why are you so calm regarding all this stuff Lin? I don't get it. You used to be rattled and upset at everything, now you are indifferent. Did you win the lottery or something?"

"Something like that Peter," Lin said with a smile. "Let's get back to the grind, shall we?"

"I guess," Peter said hesitantly.

"By the way Peter, everyone wants to know, what's up with the beard? You look like a hobo."

Peter bought a few cookies for the secretaries on his way out.

Wavering in his commitment to the lab, Peter had drafted and sent an official letter requesting a raise. It served as a sort of ultimatum. He felt that if they didn't give him one then he would have an opening to do something he actually wanted with his life. Despite his errors, Peter's leverage was due to the fact that he was the highest trained medical technologist in the Reno area. Soon, perhaps the highest paid as well.

17

The Verdict

Bill left the remote vacation ranch early to check the status of everything. Anxious to get into cell phone range to hear his voicemails, Bill drove down the freeway looking at his *iPhone* for signal bars. "There we go." A little *3G* icon popped up on the screen.

The first voicemail he opted to listen to was from Jacob's (415) San Francisco area code phone number.

"Hello, Mr. Dunlap, this is Jacob Simmons. I have completed the audit on your laboratory business in Reno. My recommendations will be sent to you via e-mail this morning. Have a great day," he said in a pleasantly professional, yet neutral voice.

Immediately, Bill opened the e-mail and saw the report downloading on his little screen.

"The verdict is in!" Bill yelled to himself in his dirty *Escalade*. "This is do or die!"

His hands shook a little bit, knowing that the course of his future was written in this little *PDF* file. "Here we go," he said as it slowly opened it up on his handheld device.

He must have felt much like a patient, anxiously awaiting news from the lab to see if the disease was terminal or not. The tables had turned on Bill. Now it was he who was at the mercy of another. He wasn't accustomed to this helpless role.

The first few pages were mere formalities, disclaimers, and niceties. He skipped through them quickly. Underlined and in bold was written:

> ***I respectfully recommend a no-buy.***

"S—t!" Bill yelled again. A semi-tractor trailer blazed by his pulled-over SUV on the I-15 highway. "I paid $20,000 for this damn audit!" Composing himself, he saw the no-buy recommendation was followed with a simple bullet-point explanation:

- *Unacceptable financial controls*

- *Unacceptable cost controls*

- *Unacceptable risk controls*

- *Unacceptable quality controls*

- *Under reinvestment in equipment and infrastructure*

- *$50,000,000 pending lawsuit with only $25,000,000 in insurance cover*

His heart sank into his stomach when reading the last item. Bill suspected that Maria disclosed the lawsuit. Since it was too early in the morning to call her, Bill listened to her series of voicemails for the week.

The last one said, *"Bill, it's Maria. I promise I can turn this lab around. We can get a total quality management system in place, set up a budget, and get everything under control. Please don't fire anyone . . . I'm confident we won't let you down."*

Shaken up emotionally, Bill got out of his stuffy *Escalade* to get some fresh air. When he looked up, lo and behold, he was parked right under a *Mulliger & Jensen* billboard:

> *Victim of malpractice? Want to be a millionaire?*
>
> *Give Mulliger and Jensen a call.*
>
> *...Jackpot!*

Outraged at the bitter irony, Bill took out his revolver and shot six .45 caliber rounds at the billboard.

Carole King's "It's Too Late" track was playing on the radio on the slow drive back to Barb at the anniversary ranch. A morning stop at any random casino bar was warranted. With his stomach churning, he looked in the rear view

148

mirror and noticed his eyes were red and watery. This was a stinging defeat.

18

Lake Tahoe Jackpot

Jacob was also driving on the freeway that morning, listening to news radio nonsense. Unfortunately, he was still stuck with his rented *Pontiac* for the drive to Lake Tahoe. His *Blackberry* beckoned him. It was his manager back at headquarters.

"Jake, I read this report . . . good work. I promise we wouldn't have sent you if we had known about that lawsuit."

"It's fine. Thank that Staten Island paralegal, Valerina, for finding it."

"So, what's the real story? Anything of value?"

Since these types of contracts stipulate that whatever the consultants find regarding the market or industry is theirs to keep, they can use it any way they want.

"Lawsuit aside, I think Bill has a 50 percent chance of salvaging the lab, but he would have to invest a lot of time and money, and I don't think he has the stomach for it. Even if they turn it around, I think *Quest Diagnostics* or *LabCorp* will eventually swallow up this lab's market share within a couple of years, or even a few months, with the way things are going."

When he finally arrived to Lake Tahoe, Jacob checked to make sure his *Blackberry* still had a signal. He put on headphones and pulled out a special CD, Otis Redding's album, "The Dock of the Bay". The fishing rod and sublime view seemed especially empty for some reason.

Knowing full well that he left the lab staff confused and frightened for their jobs, he begin to feel like his M&A audit career was a cruel path. For just a moment, Jacob felt swayed to take a different role at the firm, maybe turn around management consulting. M&A was where he could earn the most, however, and for accountants, that's an acutely important factor.

Just then, his phone rang. It was his friend from Houston, giving him an update on the lab's owned oil lease.

"Are you sure?" Jacob asked while putting down his fishing gear. "Okay, I'll check my e-mail right now."

He jumped into his car and drove to a massive log cabin estate on the lake. The gated community security guard asked Jacob who he was here to see. "I'm a guest of Mr. Mulliger," Jacob politely replied.

"Mr. Simmons?" the guard inquired.

"Yes, that's me." The gate lifted up, and Jacob drove into the elaborate estate grounds, parking his out-of-place rental car by the fountain.

The principle of seizing every possible revenue-generating opportunity wasn't just something he preached to clients. Jacob felt no alliance to anyone but himself. Maria, Bill, the firm management—they were all bidders for Mr. Simmons' valuable time.

"So, tell me, Jacob. What exactly am I able to squeeze from this piece of junk lab, and how can I take it with the least amount of effort?" Mulliger leaned in and asked.

"The real appraised value I have determined is $51.2 million, Mr. Mulliger. The lab is a mess, but is sitting on a massive oil lease royalty worth about $50 million, depending on the current spot oil price."

"Continue on," Mulliger said, not displaying the least bit of emotion from the news.

"Well, sir, the royalty holding company is ripe and ready for you to take because it's 100 percent owned by the lab."

"Please continue," Mulliger said, leading them to his trophy room.

"It looks like Bill's greatest blind spot was what his father really left him—a fortune. He was so caught up in draining the lab of pennies that he forgot to see the pound."

"So I hear," Mulliger said with a smile. Together, they smoked cigars and laughed in the trophy room.

"I presume you knew about this oil all along," Jacob inquired of Mulliger. "How did you find out?"

"You know the saying, Jacob, *a master never reveals his secret.*"

"Fair enough. So will happen to Bill?" Jacob asked while Mulliger was writing his check (it was double the size of his monthly salary and Bill's retainer, combined). Mulliger stood up and handed it to him.

"He reminds me of the elk I shot this last weekend," Mulliger said in a cold, deviant tone.

Jacob looked at all the animal heads in the trophy room. This guy was no joke.

DEVIANCE

They both were in deep, the only difference was that one did this kind of thing for a living.

Mulliger was so far away from virtue that the word's very definition had shifted from sainthood to Machiavellianism.

Feeling hollow, Jacob left with his check, probing for some rationalization for his behavior. The feeling was similar to Lin's when he stood outside of the Mulliger's *Maybach*. Tahoe's sublime tranquility was suddenly dashed, so too was the brief moment with Maria where Jacob felt a glimmer of change.

Out of compassion, Jacob had helped Maria more than he was supposed to, a deviation of his duties of objectivity. Out of greed, he betrayed his client by accepting Mulliger's offer, a double agent of sorts. But most importantly, he betrayed himself, the most haunting deviation of all.

19

The Prize

The dark night wasn't over. Back at the mansion, Mulliger told his constable to serve Bill's lawyer, Barry Shapiro, with court papers regarding the Medicare suit brought by Lin. He knew Bill was on his anniversary and out of Shapiro's cell phone range.

Now, both of Bill's planks had been breached, and his lab's only escape route was blocked off by *UltraLabs'* now failed acquisition. Bill was surrounded and desperate.

The next morning, through a complex scheme, a holdings company owned secretly by Mulliger's law firm, tendered a lowball offer for the lab:

> *Offer to purchase the entire lab entity for $350,000 cash, including all current owner's equity including assets and liabilities. Deadline to accept, eight hours. Certified check enclosed.*

The rattled Shapiro had power of attorney to accept the offer, and, not knowing about the hidden oil treasure, he was desperate to get this problem off of Bill's back. Under siege, this offer was perceived as a saving grace. This was the ultimate fire sale. Bill had wanted much more, but the lab seemed like nuclear waste at this point.

Shapiro immediately responded with a sale contract signed on Bill's behalf.

> *Offer accepted.*
> *Notarized sale documents enclosed.*

Mulliger had masterfully deceived Bill into believing that the lab was virtually worthless. He had tricked Bill into losing his will to try to save it, and so he surrendered without a chase.

Suing the lab was never Mulliger's ultimate goal, especially not over some fraud case, or even a litigation. This was an acquisition, pure and simple—a perfect kill.

In the Nevada legal and business community, there is a saying "You got Mulled!" which is another of saying Bruce Mulliger had screwed you over.

UNDER NEW MANAGEMENT

On Monday morning, Maria walked into the lab with a new owner—*Western Belle Holdings Group, Inc.* A soft-voiced, pinstriped, corporate woman named Jillian Gershaw awaited her at the front.

"Hello, you must be Maria. I'm Jillian, your new boss, so to speak," she said with a welcoming voice fit for a *Pfizer* commercial.

"Oh no! Not another 'consultant'," Maria said out loud.

"Here is a letter from Mr. Barry Shapiro, Mr. Dunlap's attorney. We want this transition to be as smooth and painless as possible," she said reassuringly, touching Maria on the shoulder.

"We will be monitoring your operations here and providing assistance where we can." This was much different than Bill barking orders via cell phone. This was a corporate boss.

For all the years of loyalty that Maria had given the lab, Bill sold it away without giving her the dignity of a single text message as a heads up.

"The lab was sold?" Maria asked in utter shock.

"Yes, it was. I'm sorry to be the one to inform you, I assumed you knew," Jillian warmly said with a forced expression of compassion.

Maria had to sit down. She was now hyperventilating.

"Someone bring me some cold water!" Jillian firmly commanded to the workers sitting just outside the office door.

"So, what now? Am I fired? What's going to happen?" Maria asked in earnest, assuming Jacob foreshadowed another round of layoffs.

"To start with, I'll need to see the financials," Jillian asserted.

"Ugggghhh," Maria gasped. "Not another audit. I just had one last week!" she protested and started to sweat.

"I know this is hard Maria . . ."

Maria interrupted, "Just tell me straight up, who all will be fired?"

"Just one," Jillian said, pulling out a job termination letter. "Tell me, where does Mr. Lin Wu sit?"

HARD LANDING

Lin came in early too, sitting at his desk with a smirk on his face, as he assumed Jillian had something to do with his cunning fraud case. Suddenly, he looked up to see Maria towering over him in tears. She handed Lin the termination notice.

"I'm so sorry Lin, I'm so sorry! I swear I had nothing to do with this."

With a surprised look on his face, he took and read the letter. He protested that the firing was illegal retaliation.

"Retaliation for what?" Maria asked. "What did you do?" she asked with a deep bellow of accusation.

"Um, nothing, never mind," Lin said quickly, packing his things and excusing himself, trying to save face by concealing emotion.

Now that Mulliger knew Lin wasn't to be trusted and that the only evidence was in his hands, Lin's career was over.

His departure was expected, but not in this way. Lin always thought it would be an emotional confrontation with Maria and Bill, especially since he was supposed to be immune from retaliation as a whistle-blower.

Walking out with his box, he passed by Peter in the parking lot.

"What the hell happened, did you quit?" Peter asked.

"I can't believe I'm getting fired when it was you who made all the mistakes!" Lin yelled back at him.

Unemployed, Lin never even picked up his viola, only the phone to call Mulliger & Jensen, over and over. He had the number memorized.

After weeks of trying to contact the firm, Mulliger's paralegal finally responded with a simple note:

> Dear Mr. Wu, we unfortunately are not able to pursue your case because of the lack of evidence. We hereby withdraw from representing you.

Lin was crushed. He had lost his job, his dignity, and now the one source of hope on which he had bet everything. He was merely a pawn, sacrificed for something bigger.

In truth, there was never really any evidence of fraud. Mulliger used Lin's uploads as a front to file a suit for the sole purpose of rattling Bill and his lawyer. In flattering Lin by showing up at the concert, Lin's guard fell, and his trust peaked. He had been sacrificed like a pawn. Lin, too, had been *'Mulled.'* Lin had betrayed his wife, his employer and fellow employees, and like Jacob, himself. The only difference was Lin walked away with no golden parachute, only a completely crushed and empty soul.

REQUEST GRANTED

Back at his desk, Peter noticed a letter waiting for him. To his surprise, he actually got the raise after all. Feeling immense guilt, as Lin was just fired and it was Peter himself who made so many errors, he put the letter into his pocket swiftly as if it was stolen money.

It was a bitter-sweet moment for Peter. Kauai, Cambodia and Tibet were no longer on the horizon. That night, he shaved his beard.

20

The Man in the Mirror

Finally back from his vacation, Bill called Shapiro to receive the welcome news that the lab was sold. "You mean it's sold and finalized? Thank God!" Bill exclaimed. "What about the lawsuit?"

"It's their problem now," Shapiro said with a laugh. "I have a cashier's check for you, if you want to come by the office."

Walking to his luxury home master bathroom, Bill had a big grin as he looked in the mirror.

"Free at last!" he said to himself.

Bill, a failed wildcatter, was blind to the fact he had been sitting on a swell of oil for years. He had killed two great heirlooms with one stone:

neglect. He virtually gave his fortune away for free.

Yet, Bill would be the last ever to know such an irony. He was just glad he had a few hundred thousand to keep his lifestyle afloat for a while.

His late-night conversations with his father's ghost in the mirror were over. The lab was sold, and he would block it all from his mind for years, including the oil lease.

Bill's lab may have been a patient that came in to the hospital too late. Despite the crash course with Maria, the audit of the lab was more accurately a postmortem. It was killed, but not just because of the brilliant hunter Mulliger. The whole ecosystem was stacked against it. It was if Bill's lab was destined to fail.

THE HUNTER

Later that month, the plaintiffs in the malpractice litigation settled for exactly what insurance covered ($25 million). In the end,

Mulliger & Jensen got its 50 percent of the damages as part of the agreement with the plaintiffs.

This trophy was, in total, worth over $65 million, all for less than the retail price of his *Maybach* limo.

What becomes of the lab is up to Maria and her ability to turn things around. A possible, yet improbable undertaking that only someone of Maria's caliber could dare to pull off.

Mulliger will hold the lab few years as to avoid suspicion, and then will probably sell it to one of the *UltraLabs* of the world. If he chooses, he could liquidate it at any time, stripping its cash and oil assets, selling the remaining equipment off, and sending the whole staff home like he did Lin. The lab was only an owned asset in his vast portfolio of big game hunted over the years. He was completely detached from Maria or anything else.

In a rare sober moment, while sitting alone in his game room, the collective stare of the multiple animal heads towering over Mulliger sent a chill through his body. One animal in particular spooked him the most, the lion. For the first time, he felt it was staring back at him.

BIBLIOGRAPHY

1.   Travers, EM. Managing Costs in Clinical Laboratories. A manager's fiscal guide to laboratory cost effectiveness and productivity. McGraw-Hill, 1989. Print.

2.   Travers EM, Delahunty DC, Hunter LL, McClatchy KD, Rudar JM. Basic Cost Accounting for Clinical Services; Approved Guideline. Pennsylvania, 1998. Print.

3.   Jones BA, Bekeris LG, Nakhleh RE, Walsh MK, Valenstein PN. "Physician satisfaction with clinical laboratory services: A college of American Pathologists Q-Probes Study of 138 Institutions." Arch Pathol Lab Med 2009; 33: 38-43.

4.   Langlois MR, Wallemacq P. "The future of hospital laboratories. Position statement from the Royal Belgian Society

of Clinical Chemistry (RBSCC)." Clin ChemLab Med 2009; 47(10): 1195-1201.

5. Gras JM, Philippe M. "Application of *Six Sigma* concept in clinical laboratories: a review." Clin Chem Lab Med 2007; 45(6): 789-796.

6. Morgan B, Brown J. "Are you a master of charge capture?" Healthcare Financial Management 2005; (March): 66-72.

7. Campos J. "*Lean* lab in action." MLO 2012; (March): 26-29.

8. Shetler C, Eckhardt J, Messmer B, Adams J, Rogers B. "A *LEAN* laboratory 'goes green'." MLO 2010; (July): 26-30.

9. Blacketer J, Redman W. "Acquiring a new analyzer." MLO 2012; (April): 24-27.

10. Cooper T, Dowling M, Honeywell SF. "Penn Medicine prognosis: reduced costs, increased revenue." Revenue Cycle Strategist 2012; Feb 9(1): 1-4.

11. Wilkinson DS, Pontius A. "Consumer direct access to clinical laboratory testing: What are the critical issues?" Clinical Leadership and Management Review

2003; Nov/Dec: 358-360.

12. Valenstein PN, Walsh MK, Stankovic AK. "Accuracy of sent-out test ordering: A College of American Pathologists Q-Probes study of ordering accuracy in 97 clinical laboratories." Arch Pathol Lab Med 2008; 132: 206-210.

13. Choi J, Kim JW, S JW, Chung CK, Kim KH, Kim JH, Kim JH, Chie EK, Cho HJ, Goo JM, Lee HJ, Wee WR, Nam SM, Lim MS, Kim YA, Yang SH, Jo EM, Hwang MA, Kim WS, Lee EH, Choi SH. "Implementation of consolidated HIS: Improving quality and efficiency of healthcare." Healthcare Informatics Research 2010; 16(4): 299-304.

14. Young DS. "Earning your keep: succeeding in laboratory reimbursement." Clinical Chemistry 1998; 44(8): 1701-1712.

15. Forsman RW. "Total cost reduction in the laboratory: a team effort." J Healthcare Mater Manage 1994; 12(3): 14-5, 20, 22.

16. Latzer DB. "Total quality management: an application in a biomedical laboratory." Hosp Cost Manage Account 1997; 9(2): 1-6.

17. Cao P, Toyabe S, Kurashima S, Okada M, Akazawa K. "A modified method of activity-based costing for objectively reducing cost drivers in hospitals." Methods Inf Med 2006; 4:462-469.

18. Janssens P. "Managing the demand for laboratory testing: options and opportunities." Clinica Chimica Acta; International Journal of Clinical Chemistry 2010; 411 (21-22): 1596-1602.

19. Alonso-Cerezo MC, Martin JS, Montes MAG, de la Iglesia VM. "Appropriate utilization of laboratory tests." Clin Chem Lab Med 2009; 47 (12): 1461-1465.

20. Sunyog M. "*Lean* management and six-sigma yield big gains in hospital's immediate response laboratory: quality improvement techniques save more than $400,000." Clinical Leadership & Management Review 2004; (September):

255-258.

21. Jones JW, McCullough LB. "Medical care manifesto." J Vasc Surg 2012; 55(6): 1812-3.

22. Well A. "Laboratory medicine: a view to the future of diagnostics and training." Rinsho Byon 2012; 60(4): 312-20.

23. Manchikanti L, Ingh V, Caraway DL, Benyamin RM, Falco FJ, Hirsch JA. "Physician payment outlook for 2012: déjà vu." Pain Physician 2012; 15(1): E27-52.

24. Conn J. "Direct delivery. Rule would remove barrier between lab, patient." Mod Healthc 2011; 41(38): 12.

25. Tieman J. "Health reform and the Affordable Care Act: public perception does not match reality." Health Prog 2011; 92(4):85.

26. Holladay EB. "Bring on the future of lab medicine." MLO Med Lab Obs 2010; 42(7): 62.

27. Amendola A, Coen S, Belladonna S, Pulvirenti FR, Clemens JM, Capobianchi

MR. "Improving clinical laboratory efficiency: a time-motion evaluation of the Abbott m2000 RealTime and Roche COBAS AmpliPrep/COBAS TaqMan PCR systems for the simultaneous quantitation of HIV-1 RNA and HCV RNA." Clin Chem Lab Med 2011; 49(8): 1283-8.

28. Plebani M, Lippi G. "Is laboratory medicine a dying profession? Blessed are those who have not seen and yet have believed." Clin Biochem 2010; 43(12): 939-41.

29. Zaninoto M, Plebani M. "the 'hospital central laboratory': automation, integration and clinical usefulness." Clin Chem Lab Med 2010; 48(7): 911-7.

30. Prusa R, Doupovcova J, Warunek D, Stankovic AK. "Improving laboratory efficiencies through significant time reduction in the preanalytical phase." Clin Chem Lab Med 2010; 48(2): 293-6.

31. Briel B, Fritz F, Thiemann V, Dugas M. "Mapping turnaround times (TAT) to a

generic timeline: a systematic review of TAT definitions in clinical domains." BMC Med Inform Decis Mak 2011; 11: 34.

32. Hwang U, Baumlin K, Berman J, Chawla NK, Handel DA, Heard K, Livote E, Pines JM, Valley M, Yadav K. "Emergency department patient volume and troponin laboratory turnaround time." Acad Emerg Med 2010; 17(5): 501-7.

33. Chung HJ, Lee W, Chun S, Park HI, Min WK. "Analysis of turnaround time by subdividing three phases for outpatient chemistry specimens." Ann Clin Lab Sci 2009; 39(2): 144-9.

34. Simundic AM, Nikolac N, Miler M, Cipak A, Topic E. "Efficiency of test report delivery to the requesting physician in an outpatient setting: an observational study." Clin Chem Lab Med 2009; 47(9): 1063-6.

35. Sheppard C, Franks N, Nolte F, Fantz C. "Improving quality of patient care in an

emergency department: a laboratory perspective." Am J Clin Pathol 2008; 130(4): 573-7.

36. Hawkins RC. "Laboratory turnaround time." Clin Biochem Rev 2007; 28(4): 179-94.

37. Blow NS. "Celebrating the modern lab." Biotechniques 2012; 52(3): 123.

38. Lai WW. "Focus on laboratory organization and productivity." J Am Soc Echocardiogr 2011; 24(6): A22.

39. Williams J. "Mapping out. Strategies for revenue cycle success." Healthc Financ Manage 2010; 64(9): 119-26.

40. Arya SC, Hernandez JS, Dale JC, Bennet KE, Varkey P. "Challennges and opportunities for medical directors in pathology and laboratory medicine: standardization, integration, and innovation." Am J Clin Pathol 2010; 133(5): 819-20.

41. Erasmus RT, Zemlin AE. "Clinical audit in the laboratory." J Clin Pathol 2009; 62(7): 593-7.

42. Kershaw J. "Sustaining the future of lab medicine." MLO med Lab Obs 2008; 40(8): 52.

43. Patterson PP. " Cost accounting in hospitals and clinical laboratories: part III." Clinical Laboratory Management Review 1989; 3(3): 151-6.

44. Toye MK. "Cost-per-test analysis for the small lab." MLO Med Lab Obs 1995; 27(7): 47-50.

45. Rutledge J, Xu M, Simpson J. "Application of the Toyota production system improves core laboratory operartions." Am J Clin Pathol 2010; 133: 24-31.

46. Carpenter RB. "Laboratory cost analysis: a practical approach." Clin Lab Manage Rev 1990; 4(3): 168-77.

47. Hawker CD. "Laboratory automation: total and subtotal." Clin Lab Med 2007; 27(4): 749-70 vi.

48. Hammer DC. "Performance is reality: how is your revenue holding up?" Healthc Financ Manage 2005; 59(7): 48-56.

49. Kisner HJ. "Make versus buy: a financial perspective." Clin Leadersh Manag Rev 2003; 17(6): 328-30.

50. Shukla CS. "Lab work. A 10-step process for laying out an efficient clinical laboratory." Health Facil Manage 2010; 23(7): 23-5.

51. Grider M, Boles K. "Managing your revenue pipeline." Clinical Leadership and Management Review 2002; (Jul/Aug): 211-14.

52. Marietti C. "White coat warriors: capitation and compliance send labs into battle for survival." Healthc Inform 1999; 16(6): 43-4, 46-8.

53. "Laboratory Administration for Pathologists", CAP Press (College of American Pathologists), 2011

54. The Dark Report, < www.darkreport.com>

ABOUT THE AUTHOR

Shadi Ashrafi, M.D. is a graduate from the University of Utah School of Medicine. She went on to complete a post-doctoral research fellowship at ARUP/University of Utah, followed by a residency training program in pathology at Orlando Regional Medical Center. She has a focus and passion for laboratory medicine and management.